THE MINDFUL SCHOOL: HOW TO ASSESS AUTHENTIC LEARNING

BY KAY BURKE

IRI/Skylight Publishing, Inc.
Palatine, Illinois

The Mindful School:
How to Assess Authentic Learning
Third Printing

Published by IRI/Skylight Publishing, Inc.
200 E. Wood Street, Suite 274
Palatine, Illinois 60067
Phone 800-348-4474, 708-991-6300
FAX 708-991-6420

Creative Director: Robin Fogarty
Editors: Julia E. Noblitt, Erica Pochis
Type Compositor: Donna Ramirez
Book Designer: Michael Melasi
Graphic Designer: David Stockman
Production Coordinator: Amy Behrens

0887C-6-94D

Dedication

I dedicate this book to classroom teachers who share a new vision of assessment—a vision that emphasizes meaningful tasks instead of drills and skills; critical thinking instead of rote memorization; self-reflection instead of traditional grading scales; and thoughtful learner outcomes instead of standardized test scores.

TABLE OF CONTENTS

Foreword

"When you cannot measure it, when you cannot express it in numbers, your knowledge is of a very meager and unsatisfactory kind."— Lord Kelvin

This archaic, technological, and reductionist view expressed by the 19th-century physicist-mathematician still influences our efforts to translate educational goals into observable, measurable outcomes.

As communities work toward developing mindful schools, they also reorient their concepts about curriculum, policies, organization of time, and assessment of progress. They set aside some of their outmoded 19th-century procedures to make room for mindful practices.

Outcomes of the mindful school include:
- The capacity for continual learning
- Knowing how to behave when answers to problems are not immediately apparent
- Cooperativeness and team building
- Precise communication in a variety of modes
- Appreciation for disparate value systems
- Problem solving that requires creativity and ingenuity
- The enjoyment of resolving ambiguous, paradoxical, and discrepant situations
- The generation and organization of an overabundance of technologically produced information

Growth toward these goals of the mindful school requires new, more authentic and appropriate forms of assessment. We cannot employ product-oriented assessment techniques to assess achievement of these process-oriented outcomes. Norm-referenced standardized test scores alone give us authentic numbers that reflect the achievement and performance of isolated skills at a particular moment in time. All of the outcomes above, however, are dynamic, experiential, and emotionally charged. They incorporate the feelings of mastery in problem solving and the energizing power of discovery.

In this volume, Kay Burke has collected a wide range of alternative forms of assessment. She presents them in a meaningful and practical format, which makes their use easily applicable to those in schools and classrooms searching for more authentic forms of assessment. They will prove valuable to teaching teams wishing to collect data to evaluate their curriculum and instructional decision making. They will assist in communicating more thoughtfully to parents. Most importantly, they will signal to students that self-assessment is the ultimate goal of the mindful school.

The format of her presentation builds conceptual understandings and practical applications of assessment strategies. Furthermore, her mode of presentation models how students, teachers, administrators, and parents might work together to gather data to reflect on, and communicate achievements of, the outcomes of the mindful school.

Kay cautions us that while all the forms of assessment have merit, no one technique is adequate in assessing all the outcomes of the mindful school. Having a range and a variety of strategies will more likely yield usable information, provide for a diversity of styles, and allow for a greater number of situations in which students may express their learning.

As Jacob Viner states, "When you *can* measure it, when you *can* express it in numbers, your knowledge is *still* of a meager and unsatisfactory kind."

Arthur L. Costa
Professor Emeritus
California State University
Sacramento, California
August 1993

Acknowledgments

Learning is an interactive process. Throughout the past three years, I have had the pleasure to interact with and to learn from hundreds of educators throughout the United States and Canada while I conducted courses, inservices, and seminars on authentic classroom assessment. More than 250 teachers in the Field-Based Master of Arts in Teaching and Leadership Program sponsored by Saint Xavier University and IRI/Skylight in the Chicago area applied these ideas in their classes to see if they worked; they did.

Educators at the Gabbard Institute sponsored by Phi Delta Kappa in Bloomington, Indiana, and the New York State United Teachers (NYSUT) training program have provided valuable feedback during the "trial run" of the book. Together we have expanded and refined our repertoire of assessment techniques so that kindergarten to college teachers can apply the ideas with their students.

In addition to the teachers and administrators with whom I have worked, I would also like to thank the staff members at IRI/Skylight Publishing for their patience, dedication, and talent. They are all a part of a creative publishing team that is at the forefront of educational change.

I would like to give special thanks to Arthur Costa for writing the foreword to my book and for teaching me the importance of reflection and self-assessment; to Jim Bellanca for helping me connect thoughtful outcomes to the assessment process; and to Robin Fogarty for making me realize the importance of teaching and learning for transfer.

Finally, I would not have been able to balance the researching and writing of this book with my other responsibilities without the professional support of Beth Forbes and the rest of the IRI/Skylight staff and the personal support of my husband, Frank, my mother Lois Brown, and the Brown and Burke families.

The time has come to de-emphasize traditional grades and to demystify the entire grading process. We need to focus instead on the process of learning and the progress of the individual student. Poor test-takers everywhere should know that the time has come to find out what they really know and can do—rather than how well they take tests!

Kay Burke
August 1993

Introduction

THE CURRENT STATUS OF ASSESSMENT

"Our history is thin when it comes to standard setting and assessment. We know how to design basic skills testing; how to use test data to rank, rather than improve, schools and to sort, rather than educate, children. We have rarely developed productive, rather than reductive or punitive, assessment and accountability systems—despite the fact that our students are among the most tested in the world."
-Wolf, LeMahieu, and Eresh, 1992, p. 9

For many years student assessment has been relegated to a secondary role in the educational process. Many educators feel it has been ignored, misused, and totally misunderstood by administrators, teachers, parents, and students. In the 1990s, assessment has emerged as one of the major components in the restructured school. One cannot open an educational journal or attend a workshop without reading and hearing "alternative," "performance," or "authentic assessment."

The emergence of authentic assessment coincides with a decline in the significance of standardized testing. Almost everyone is aware of the controversy surrounding standardized tests. Charges that standardized tests do not measure significant learner outcomes, do not measure growth and development, and do not accurately reflect what students can and cannot do have been made over and over again. Yet, despite the research and the critics of standardized tests, policymakers, parents, and the general public base much of their perception of the educational system on the publication of standardized test scores and the comparisons of the scores in schools, districts, and states.

PAUSE

In the 1990s, assessment has emerged as one of the major components in the restructured school.

Standardized and Teacher-Made Tests

Standardized testing has been debated and scrutinized in the media and in school board meetings on a regular basis over the past twenty years. What has not been reported nearly as often, however, is that standardized tests do *not* play a big role in classroom assessment, other than being used for school-wide tracking or placement. Most grades students receive are given by classroom teachers and are based on the work students do in the classroom. These class grades constitute the majority of grades and have always been assigned by teachers—teachers, who, unfortunately, have had little or no training in tests and measurements. "Educators who have long protested the misuse of standardized tests must concede that most of the tests students take are devised by teachers, and that some of those are even worse than the published ones" (Brandt, 1992b, p. 7).

Assessment has long been the "missing link" in effective school programs. Teachers who introduce exciting educational strategies like cooperative learning, higher-order thinking skills, multiple intelligences, and integrated curricula challenge students to expand their thinking and stretch their creativity. Their teaching signals a new order of change and challenge, but when they end the unit with a multiple-choice test, their assessment signals a return to tradition. It does not take long for students to figure out how to study and what to value. If teachers teach what they think is important, then they need to test what they think is important.

Assessment Training for Teachers

Hills (1991) blames the classroom assessment problem on the lack of training teachers receive. Only four states require prospective teachers to take a course on evaluation. Most colleges of education offer courses in evaluation, but few students take them. Hills also laments the fact that few students in the evaluation courses he has taught are able to construct test items that are clear, high-level, and related to course outcomes.

Stiggins (1985) agrees that pre-service teacher training in colleges of education often fails to include a course on testing and rarely do teachers receive inservice training on effective assessment techniques once they are employed. He feels that if teachers enter the profession with little or no training in testing and measurement, they are unlikely to get that training along the way.

PAUSE

If teachers teach what they think is important, then they need to test what they think is important.

"Our current assessment values may also be contributing to inadequate daily assessment of student achievement in some classrooms. Since we have rarely inquired into the quality of teacher-developed tests, offered training in classroom assessment, or included classroom assessment in the principal's leadership role, we simply do not know how well teachers measure student achievement or how to help them if they need help" (Stiggins, 1985, p. 72).

Hills also criticizes teachers who allow discipline to enter into assessment. Students who do not bring their pencil, book, or homework to class or who get caught cheating on tests often get zeros or "Fs" on work. Other teachers assign zeros for late work. These zeros are then averaged together to arrive at a final grade. It takes only a few nonacademic zeros to result in a D or F for the term. Hills feels that "grades should *not* be used for disciplinary purposes. If a grade is altered as a way of inflicting punishment, it no longer accurately reflects academic achievement, and its proper meaning is destroyed" (Hills, 1991, p. 541).

Role of Administrators

The role school administrators play in setting standards for classroom assessments and monitoring their effectiveness is minimal. Like classroom teachers, most administrators have had little or no training in assessment themselves; therefore, they cannot provide the guidance to help teachers develop and use appropriate assessments that can meet the needs of all of the students (Hills, 1991).

Observation checklists of teacher performance rarely include categories for assessment. It is not uncommon to have good teachers create ambiguous assessments that do not measure what was taught and that penalize poor test-takers or poor readers. These teachers do not mean to cause students to feel insecure, to lower their self-esteem, or to fail, but they just do not know how to test. Administrators, therefore, need to assume a more proactive role by working with teachers to construct meaningful assessments and to prevent teachers from using academic grades to control student behavior.

Grade, If You Must

Grades are, unfortunately, an integral part of the American educational system. As early as kindergarten, students receive grades that

PAUSE

Like classroom teachers, most administrators have had little or no training in assessment....

they might not even understand. Ask any teacher what he or she hates most about teaching, and there's a good chance it's "giving grades." Many a teacher has agonized over report cards trying to decide the fate of a student. It is a gut-wrenching task for teachers to translate everything they know about what a student knows, can do, and feels into one single letter or numerical score. That final grade may determine promotion or retention. It may determine placement in a class or school or participation in extracurricular activities. It may determine school honor roll, class ranking, college admission, college scholarship, or career placement. All of these things may be determined by a grading process that rarely guards against teachers being too lenient, rigorous, or arbitrary.

PAUSE

. . .traditional As, Bs, Cs, Ds, and Fs still dominate as the "weapon of choice" in most schools.

A great deal rides on the final evaluation of a student. Grades can affect the self-confidence, self-esteem, motivation, and future of a student. Fortunately, many school systems are moving away from traditional letter and number grades at the primary level and toward portfolios, student-led parent-teacher conferences, anecdotal records, checklists, multiple scores, and other more authentic de-scriptors of a student's progress. But despite the new attempts to restructure report cards to reflect the emphasis on performance, social skills, higher-order thinking, and other meaningful outcomes, traditional As, Bs, Cs, Ds, and Fs still dominate as the "weapon of choice" in most schools. With the stroke of a pen or the "bubble" of a scantron computer sheet, a teacher can pass judgment on a stu-dent. "It [a grade] marks the lives of those who receive it. It may not be imprinted on the forehead, but it certainly leaves an impression" (Majesky, 1993, p. 88). The grade can become the scarlet letter of Puritan days if it is based on trivial tasks or a student's behavior, absentee pattern, attitude, neatness, parental pressure, punctuality, or personality.

"As at the last judgment, students are sorted into the wheat and the chaff. Rewards of A's and B's go out to the good, and punishments of F's are doled out to the bad. 'Gifts' of D's (D's are always gifts) are meted out, and C's (that wonderfully tepid grade) are bestowed on those whose names teachers can rarely remember" (Majesky, 1993, p. 88).

Hopefully, the restructured school will make assessment part of instruction rather than separate from it. And Majesky's scenario of the last judgment of branding students with grades will be as out-dated as the mimeograph machine.

Traditional Cognitive Science

The methods of assessment used in schools are often determined by beliefs about learning. Early theories of learning indicated that educators needed to use a "building-blocks-of-knowledge" approach whereby students acquired complex higher-order skills by breaking learning down into a series of skills. Every skill had a prerequisite skill, and it was assumed that after the basic skills were learned, they could be assembled into more complex thinking and insight. Therefore, students who scored poorly on standardized tests at an early age would usually be assigned to the "remedial" or "basic skills" classes so they could master those essential basic skills before being exposed to the more challenging and motivating complex thinking skills.

Students who have trouble memorizing basic skills out of context are often labeled slow learners. Unfortunately, some of these students become so bored and frustrated with year after year of drill-and-skill work, that they never develop the thinking skills needed to solve real-world problems. Since they rarely have the opportunity to receive a motivating and challenging curriculum or discover knowledge for themselves, they often become behavior problems or dropouts. Statistics suggest that in the United States one student drops out of school every eight seconds of the school day. According to the U.S. Department of Education, ten states have high school dropout rates over thirty percent (Hodgkinson, 1991). Apparently, many students choose either to "act out" or "drop out" rather than endure the monotonous drill-and-skill cycle.

"Current evidence about the nature of learning makes it apparent that instruction which strongly emphasizes structured drill and practice on discrete, factual knowledge does students a major disservice. Learning isolated facts and skills is more difficult without meaningful ways to organize the information and make it easy to remember" (North Central Regional Educational Laboratory, 1991a, p. 10).

Constructivist Theories of Learning

In the constructivist's view, "learning is a constructive process in which the learner is building an internal representation of knowledge, a personal interpretation of experience. This representation is constantly open to change... Learning is an active process in which meaning is developed on the basis of experience" (Bednar, Cunningham, Duffy, and Perry, 1993, p. 5).

PAUSE

"...instruction which strongly emphasizes structured drill and practice on discrete, factual knowledge does students a major disservice."
-NCREL, 1991a, p. 10

Constructivists suggest that learning is *not* linear. It does not occur on a timeline of basic skills. Instead, learning occurs at a very uneven pace and proceeds in many different directions at once. The constructivists also believe that instead of learning being "decontextualized" and taught, for example, by memorizing the parts of speech, it must be situated in a rich context of writing or speaking. Real-world contexts are needed if learning is to be constructed and transferred beyond the classroom. "Conceptual learning is not something to be delayed until a particular age or until all the basic facts have been mastered. People of all ages and ability levels constantly use and refine concepts" (North Central Regional Educational Laboratory, 1991a, p. 10).

Meaningful learning does not just happen when people are able to receive information through direct instruction. In order for meaningful learning to take place, people have to interpret information and relate it to their own prior knowledge. They need to not only know *how* to perform, but also *when* to perform and how to *change* the performance to fit new and different situations (North Central Regional Educational Laboratory, 1991b). Therefore, traditional forms of assessment like multiple-choice tests can only assess lower-order recall of factual information and one or two of the multiple intelligences. These tests are rarely able to assess whether or not students can organize complex problems. The new cognitive perspective stresses that meaningful learning is constructive. Learners should be able to construct meaning for themselves, reflect on the significance of the meaning, and self-assess to determine their own strengths and weaknesses. Integrated curricula, cooperative learning, problem-based learning, and whole language are just a few examples of curricula that help students construct knowledge for themselves.

New assessments, therefore, should focus not on whether or not students can acquire knowledge, but whether or not they can acquire the disposition to *use* the skills and strategies and apply them appropriately. Recent studies suggest that poor thinkers and problem solvers may *possess* the skills they need, but may fail to *use* them in certain tasks. Integration of learning, motivation, collaboration, the affective domain, and metacognitive skills all contribute to lifelong learning. Assessment practices must stop measuring knowledge skills and start measuring the disposition to *use* the skills (North Central Regional Educational Laboratory, 1991b).

PAUSE

In order for meaningful learning to take place, people have to interpret information and relate it to their own prior knowledge.

Authentic Achievement

Archbald and Newmann (1988) believe that before educators try to *assess* authentically, they should make sure they *teach* authentically. Authentic academic achievement is a prerequisite to authentic assessment. They believe that achievement tasks should meet at least three criteria: disciplined inquiry, integration of knowledge, and value beyond evaluation.

Disciplined inquiry depends on prior knowledge, an in-depth understanding of a problem, and a move beyond knowledge produced by others to a formulation of new ideas. History students can go to primary sources to research generalizations made in the textbooks to form their own conclusions. Science students can develop, perform, and report on their experiments. Through disciplined inquiry, students can respond to and sometimes even reject the public knowledge base.

Integration of knowledge requires students to consider things as "whole" rather than fragments or "factoids." Tests often test students' knowledge of unrelated facts, definitions, or events. Students may memorize the short answers, but they do not see the whole picture. For example, knowing all the parts of a sentence does not mean one can write a sentence. Archbald and Newmann believe that students "must also be involved in the production, not simply the reproduction, of new knowledge, because this requires knowledge integration" (1988, p. 3). Authentic classroom tasks, therefore, prepare students for life, not just a test.

The last criterion for authentic achievement is that it has some value beyond evaluation. "When people write letters, news articles, insurance claims, poems; when they speak a foreign language; when they develop blueprints; when they create a painting, a piece of music, or build a stereo cabinet, they demonstrate achievements that have a special value missing in tasks contrived only for the purpose of assessing knowledge (such as spelling quizzes, laboratory exercises, or typical final exams)" (Archbald & Newmann, 1988, p. 3).

Archbald and Newmann (1988) also believe that it is important that the tasks assigned have some value outside of the classroom. If students are to apply the in-school tasks to life, they need to perform or produce the skills in school. They also need "flexible time" be-

PAUSE

Disciplined inquiry depends on prior knowledge, an in-depth understanding of a problem, and a move beyond knowledge produced by others to a formulation of new ideas.

cause the real world does not force people to produce or solve problems in fifty-minute class periods. Bell schedules may help manage large numbers of teenagers, but it does not help students learn. Many school systems are moving to block schedules to allow students more time to focus on authentic tasks.

Another factor that is necessary for achieving authentic achievement is collaboration. Even though schools usually focus on students working alone, the real world allows and encourages people to talk, ask questions, get help, and receive feedback. Denying students the right to cooperate and collaborate diminishes the authenticity of the achievement. Unless there are some fundamental changes in the nature of schooling itself, students will not see the connection between school and their own lives nor will they be motivated to be lifelong learners.

Equally important for authentic achievement is a re-examination of the curriculum. In this age of the information explosion, it is impossible to "cover the curriculum" because there are too many facts and too much material. Instead of allowing students to interact with and process information, teachers are tackling too much information too superficially. Educators need to practice what Costa calls "selective abandonment" and eliminate the trivial, the boring, and the inane! Prioritize what is really important and develop clear standards to measure achievement. "Less is more" as Gertrude Stein supposedly advised a young Ernest Hemingway. Educators must ask themselves, "What is really important for our students to know now and still know twenty-five years from now?"

Assessment and Evaluation

Assessment is the process of *gathering* evidence of what a student can do. Evaluation is the process of *interpreting* the evidence and *making judgments* and decisions based on it. If the assessment is not sound, the evaluation will not be sound. In most classrooms, teachers *assess* a student on the basis of observations, oral conversations, and written work. They make instructional decisions based on these assessments. If the assessment is ongoing and frequent, changes can be made immediately to help the student achieve the desired outcome. If the assessment is flawed or sporadic, the evaluation will come at the end of the unit, quarter, or semester—often too late to help the student before the final grade or end of the term.

PAUSE

Unless there are some fundamental changes in the nature of schooling itself, students will not see the connection between school and their own lives nor will they be motivated to be lifelong learners.

Jeroski says that "evaluation is much more than a way of monitoring change—it is the single most powerful way in which teachers communicate their values and beliefs to students, parents, and colleagues. The way we look at evaluation is connected to the way we look at and interact with the world around us" (Jeroski, 1992, p. 281).

Since what a student knows is always changing, assessment of what a student knows should be based on comparisons taken over a period of time. The purposes of assessment are many. Policymakers use assessment to set standards, monitor the quality of education, and formulate policies. Administrators use assessment to monitor the effectiveness of a program, identify program strengths and weaknesses, and designate priorities. Teachers use assessment to make grouping decisions, diagnose strengths and weaknesses, evaluate curriculum, give feedback, and determine grades. Parents and students use assessment to gauge student progress and make informed decisions about college and careers (North Central Regional Educational Laboratory, 1991b).

Diagnostic Evaluation

Diagnostic evaluation is often done at the beginning of a course, quarter, semester, or year to assess the skills, abilities, interests, levels of achievement, or difficulties of one student or a class. Diagnostic evaluation should be done informally; therefore, it should never be used for a grade. Teachers can use the results to modify programs, determine causes of learning difficulties, and to see at what level a student enters a class. By having information about the student's entry-level skills, a teacher can assess how far the student has progressed throughout the course or year (Board of Education for the City of Etobicoke, 1987).

Formative Evaluation

Formative evaluations are conducted continually throughout the year. They are used to monitor students' progress and provide meaningful and immediate feedback as to what students have to do to achieve thoughtful outcomes; their purpose is to improve instruction rather than grade students. Too much emphasis has been placed on the summative or end evaluation where it is discovered what the student does and doesn't know—often too late to do anything about it. Testing has always been *separate* from learning. Instead, assessment should be an integral part of the learning process—an ongoing part. The results of the formative evaluation can be used to redirect

PAUSE

Since what a student knows is always changing, assessment of what a student knows should be based on comparisons taken over a period of time.

efforts, provide information, evaluate the program, and form the basis for the final summative evaluation (Board of Education for the City of Etobicoke, 1987).

"The concept that testing is initiated externally from the student, separate from the learning process, and primarily aimed at determining whether inert knowledge is in students' short-term memories exercises far too much influence over school people today. The goals of thoughtfulness are that students internalize capacities to evaluate their learning, do so as they learn, and do so in ways that exhibit their capacity to be *performing* thinkers, problem solvers, and inquirers" (Brown, 1989, p. 115).

Summative Evaluation

"Summative evaluation occurs at the end of a unit, activity, course, term or program. It is used with formative evaluation to determine student achievement and program effectiveness" (Board of Education for the City of Etobicoke, 1987, p. 9).

This type of evaluation reports the degree to which course objectives or outcomes have been met. It can also be used to report to parents, promote or retain, measure student achievement, and measure program effectiveness.

Some Definitions of Authentic Assessment

Many terms or phrases are used when discussing the alternatives to conventional, multiple-choice testing. Alternative assessment, authentic assessment, and performance-based assessment are used sometimes synonymously "to mean variants of performance assessments that require students to generate rather than choose a response" (Herman, Aschbacher, and Winters, 1992, p. 2). Stefonek has gathered the following definitions and phrases from experts in the field to help describe authentic assessment:

- Methods that emphasize learning and thinking, especially higher-order thinking skills such as problem-solving strategies (Collins)
- Tasks that focus on students' ability to produce a quality product or performance (Wiggins)
- Disciplined inquiry that integrates and produces knowledge, rather than reproduces fragments of information others have discovered (Newmann)

PAUSE

Many terms or phrases are used "to mean variants of performance assessments that require students to generate rather than choose a response."
-Herman, Aschbacher, and Winters, 1992, p. 2

- Meaningful tasks at which students should learn to excel (Wiggins)
- Challenges that require knowledge in good use and good judgment (Wiggins)
- A new type of positive interaction between the assessor and assessee (Wiggins)
- An examination of differences between trivial school tasks (e.g., giving definitions of biological terms) and more meaningful performance in nonschool settings (e.g., completing a field survey of wildlife) (Newmann)
- Involvement that demystifies tasks and standards (Wiggins)
                                                    (Stefonek, 1991, p. 1)

Regardless of the different terminology, most of the various definitions exhibit two central features: "First, all are viewed as *alternatives* to traditional multiple-choice, standardized achievement tests; second, all refer to *direct* examination of student *performance* on significant tasks that are relevant to life outside of school" (Worthen, 1993, p. 445).

Authentic assessment means many things to many people, but Archbald and Newmann perhaps say it best: "A valid assessment system provides information about the particular tasks on which students succeed or fail, but more important, it also presents tasks that are worthwhile, significant, and meaningful—in short, *authentic*" (Archbald & Newmann, 1988, p. 1).

Accountability Testing

In addition to the assessments created and evaluated by teachers in the classroom, many states are implementing large-scale accountability testing that includes traditional standardized tests as well as some of the new performance-based standardized tests created by testing services and states.

Cole describes the differences between measurement to serve accountability and policy goals and measurement for instructional purposes. (See chart on following page.)

In some states, large-scale accountability takes the form of an exhibition, a portfolio, or a performance test, where all students are evaluated according to a systematized scale. O'Neil (1992) says that some states like Kentucky, California, and Vermont are moving toward their own

PAUSE

"A valid assessment system. . .also presents tasks that are worthwhile, significant, and meaningful— in short, *authentic.*"
-Archbald & Newmann, 1988, p.1

Large-Scale Assessment to Serve Accountability and Policy Goals	Classroom Assessment to Support Instruction
1. Formal 2. Objective 3. Time-efficient 4. Cost-effective 5. Widely applicable 6. Centrally processed (adapted from Cole in Shepard, 1989, p. 7)	1. Informal 2. Teacher-mandated 3. Adapted to local content 4. Locally scored 5. Sensitive to short-term change in students' knowledge 6. Meaningful to students 7. Immediate and detailed feedback 8. Tasks that have instructional value 9. Conducted in a climate of greater trust than standardized tests

PAUSE

Some experts worry that the new acountability tests may be oversold and educators will rush to replace one type of flawed standardized test with another type of flawed performance-based test.

wide-scale accountability programs. Other state offices are waiting to see how pilot programs go before they make the financial and time commitment to start their own programs. Some experts worry that the new accountability tests may be oversold and educators will rush to replace one type of flawed standardized test with another type of flawed performance-based test. O'Neil states that testing officials must also decide if state assessment programs can use the tests for accountability purposes *and* for improvement of classroom instruction.

Aschbacher warns that "performance assessments could suffer from some of the same problems of standardized tests if the same high stakes are applied to them" (O'Neil, 1992, p. 19). He is also concerned about using these tests for high-stake accountability while they are still being developed. Using these new tests to evaluate students at this point could result in a lot of criticism, confusion, and embarrassment—not to mention lawsuits.

Classroom assessments, on the other hand, are conducted in a climate of greater trust and relaxation than standardized tests. Classroom observations and grades do not have to meet the same standards of accuracy. "Errors made in judging individual students are less serious and more easily redressed as teachers gather new evidence. Although single teacher tests are probably less reliable (in a statistical sense) than a one-hour standardized test, accumulation of data gathered about individual pupils in the course of a school year has much more accuracy" (Shepard, 1989, p. 7).

Stiggins wonders why it is necessary to make a choice between traditional and standardized tests and classroom assessments. "One of the things that troubles me greatly is that we're setting up performance assessments and paper-and-pencil tests against one another. Each test has a contribution to make. We can't throw away any of the tools at our disposal" (O'Neil, 1992, p. 19). Critics of standardized tests want to throw out the baby with the bath water. Why can't we use all the tools at our disposal to assess students fairly, accurately, and authentically?

And Now. . . the Tools!

As Stiggins noted, educators need all the tools at their disposal to assess students. Authentic classroom assessments provide teachers with a *repertoire* of tools to measure student growth. The following twelve chapters focus on specific tools teachers need to create a vivid, colorful, and true moving picture of a student as he or she develops and grows over the course of a year. In the past a student's progress was chronicled by a superficial "picture" of a student. The picture usually consisted of a few snapshots of standardized test scores, midterms, final grades, and other one-dimensional scores that lay lifeless in the permanent record file seen by some, used by few, and appreciated by none.

One could only guess at what that student thought about, what skills he or she came to class with, and what skills he or she left with. Nothing more than a static glimpse of a student can be gleaned from the traditional cumulative record system of the past two centuries.

A more vivid image of the student of the twenty-first century is emerging in the authentic classroom. Instead of a flat, one-dimensional "picture" in a folder, teachers can capture the vitality, movement, and physical and mental growth of a student in a moving, three-dimensional "video."

The "video" is colorful, alive, and fluid. One can see students develop, change, and grow in every frame. And what's more important, students see themselves develop, change, and grow. At the end of the year, parents, teachers, and students can see and hear learning and evaluate more effectively what has been achieved and what goals still await.

Each chapter will introduce a new tool to "videotape" each student's growth. The chapters include a description of "What is the tool?" "Why should we use the tool?" and "How should we use the tool?" Examples

PAUSE

"One of the things that troubles me greatly is that we're setting up performance assessments and paper-and-pencil tests against one another."
-O'Neil, 1992, p. 19

of many of the assessments are provided and teachers will get a chance to create original tools on the "On Your Own" page at the end of each chapter, as well as self-evaluate their work on the "Reflection Page." These are just a few of the many options available for teachers to add to their repertoire of assessment strategies as they turn on the power, push the "play" button, and prepare to "videotape" a student in motion, a student who is a lifelong learner.

Cathy reviews, self-evaluates, and reflects on her own video performances as she plans for her future.

THOUGHTFUL OUTCOMES

> "Many educational
> programs do not have
> clearly defined
> purposes."
>
> -Tyler, 1949, p. 3

WHAT ARE THOUGHTFUL OUTCOMES?

Ralph W. Tyler began chapter one of his book, *Basic Principles of Curriculum and Instruction,* with the quotation on the previous page— "Many educational programs do not have clearly defined purposes." The book was originally published in 1949 as the syllabus for the Education 360 course at the University of Chicago. The four fundamental questions that Tyler said must be answered in developing any curriculum and plan of instruction are as critical now as they were when he wrote the book more than four decades ago.

FOUR FUNDAMENTAL QUESTIONS FOR CURRICULUM DEVELOPMENT

1. What educational purposes should the school seek to attain?
2. What educational experiences can be provided that are likely to attain these purposes?
3. How can these educational experiences be effectively organized?
4. How can we determine whether these purposes are being attained?

–Tyler, 1949, p. 1

Tyler said that all aspects of the educational program are really means to accomplish these basic educational purposes. The educational objectives are, hopefully, based on wise judgment. Since "education is a process of changing the behavior patterns of people... it is clear that educational objectives, then, represent the kinds of changes in behavior that an educational institution seeks to bring about in its students" (Tyler, 1949, pp. 5–6).

Precursor to Outcomes
King and Evans feel that Tyler's course syllabus was a precursor of outcome-based education (OBE): "Tyler noted the importance of the *objective* for systematically planning educational experiences, stating

that a well-written objective should identify both the behavior to be developed in the student and 'the area of content or of life in which the behavior is to be applied'" (King & Evans, 1991, p. 73).

What Are Outcomes?

The work by Tyler, Bloom, and his colleagues in developing objectives for cognitive and affective domains, and of Mager in developing behavior objectives, have led educators to the term "outcomes." The word "outcome" is used interchangeably with "goal," "purpose," "demonstration of learning," "culmination," and "end."

Spady, Filby, and Burns (1986) describe exit outcomes as "competencies, knowledge, and orientations." They are the "end-products" of the entire instructional process. Outcomes can include internal changes in the learner or observable changes. For example, one exit outcome might be that students become collaborative workers who cooperate effectively with a diversity of people.

Outcome-Based Education (OBE)

Based on this definition, "an outcome-based program requires a change in traditional approaches to curriculum development, shifting the focus from objectives derived often from content or textbook outlines to objectives based on desired changes in the learner" (King & Evans, 1991, p. 73). OBE has emerged in the 1990s during a decade of concern by parents, business people, and politicians about accountability. One of its major goals is to make sure all students learn what is really important so they can be successful after they leave school.

The key words to describe outcomes are "significant," "meaningful," and "thoughtful." School districts across the country are developing significant or essential learning outcomes that all students are expected to achieve. "All students can learn and succeed (but not on the same day in the same way)" (Spady & Marshall, 1991, p. 67).

Many school districts do not subscribe to the total OBE program, but whether or not districts or schools label the restructuring of their goals as purposes, ends, objectives, or outcomes, most of them are attempting to follow the guidelines established by Tyler. They know it is important to establish educational purposes before they select the content, the implementation strategies, and the evaluation program.

PAUSE

School districts across the country are developing significant or essential learning outcomes that all students are expected to achieve.

PAUSE

"Transforming education from a process that emphasizes inputs to one that stresses outcomes could be more complex than educators and policy makers realize."
-Pipho, 1992, p. 662

Controversy About Outcomes

The term "learner outcomes" sometimes refers to performance-based assessment, authentic assessment, exhibitions, or portfolios of student work. Such portfolios emphasize what a student can demonstrate rather than how he or she takes tests. "The terminology may differ...but states and school districts are increasingly moving to adopt new programs that could change testing, teaching, and learning. Transforming education from a process that emphasizes inputs to one that stresses outcomes could be more complex than educators and policy makers realize" (Pipho, 1992, p. 662). Pipho worries about the lack of the public's understanding of why all of a sudden standardized testing that comes from "outside" the school to check up on students and teachers is being replaced by assessment taking place "inside" the school. Instead of external testing, students progress through school by demonstrating outcomes. In 1992, the State of Pennsylvania abolished the Carnegie Unit requirements for high school graduation. The ruling stipulates that students demonstrate state learning outcomes and local outcomes specified in the district's strategic plan and that they complete an individual or group research, writing, or other project in at least one area of study.

Pipho agrees that the intentions are admirable, but he says that a great deal of planning and public relations work needs to be done to educate the parents and the community. He says some parents are confused as to how students can be held to standards that are not yet clearly spelled out. For example, one of Pennsylvania's outcomes is appreciation and understanding of others, and parents are concerned that the state will be introducing and assessing values (Pipho, 1992). It is evident that educators and community members must discuss the outcomes and communicate their feelings and opinions during the outcome planning process.

Simplicity, Simplicity, Simplicity!

Simplicity is sometimes lost on proponents of outcome-based education. One Colorado school district changed traditional report cards to a new report card with ninety-five holistic categories and no grades. Parents, however, persuaded school officials to restore letter grades in some subjects. "One parent was quoted as saying that the report cards are written in 'edubabble,' a form of language only educators can understand" (Pipho, 1992, p. 663). Eliminating traditional high school graduation requirements and report cards in favor of outcome-based assessment may be a new revolution in teaching, but Pipho warns that much more effort needs to be spent "crafting educational outcomes that are both simple and effective" and "acceptance by the public (including those on the political right), by colleges and universities, and by rank-and-file teachers is needed before 'outcomes education' will become a household phrase" (Pipho, 1992, p. 663).

WHY DO WE NEED THOUGHTFUL OUTCOMES?

Despite the controversy about replacing grades or eliminating Carnegie Units or course requirements, most educators feel that establishing significant learner outcomes prior to creating a curriculum is imperative. Discovering what a student can do via a diagnostic test or some criterion-referenced measurement also provides baseline data that will be necessary later to see how much the student has improved on a continuum of tasks. Significant outcomes focus on the "big picture" instead of discrete facts, rote memorization, or decontextualized bits of information.

In 1949, Tyler lamented the fact that students memorized information they did not understand and forgot information at a very rapid rate. "Typically students will have forgotten 50 percent of the information they acquire within a year after completing a course, and 75 percent within two years after completing a course" (Tyler, 1949, p. 73). He suggested that one way to help students retain what they learn is to let them investigate their own interests. The interests can be used as a focus of educational attention and as a way to achieve the thoughtful outcomes.

"Education is an active process. It involves the active efforts of the learner himself. In general, the learner learns only those things which he does" (Tyler, 1949, p. 11). Active learning allows students to construct knowledge for themselves and master skills for today that they will still use twenty-five years from now. Much of the content students learn in school will be obsolete twenty-five years from now; therefore, learning *how* to learn is probably more important than deciding *what* to learn. Moreover, the knowledge base is increasing so quickly that students will not be able to learn content for today, much less retain the content for the future.

PAUSE

Significant outcomes focus on the "big picture" instead of discrete facts, rote memorization, or decontextualized bits of information.

One important aspect of outcome-based education is the realization that not all students learn in the same way and at the same rate. They need expanded opportunities to develop their skills. Some of the options include cooperative learning, second-chance testing, peer tutoring, activities that appeal to different learning styles, and technology. There are high expectations for all to succeed and to produce quality work, but not all students have to achieve the same outcome at the same time.

HOW CAN WE USE THOUGHTFUL OUTCOMES?

Similar to the four fundamental questions that Tyler recommended curriculum developers ask before they design curriculum (see page 2), Costa and Kallick (1992) describe the three major decisions curriculum designers today need to make. First, they need to establish their outcomes or goals. Second, they need to design the delivery system by which these goals can be achieved (design, materials, time, and placement of learnings). And third, they need to develop procedures to monitor and evaluate the achievement of the goals as a result of employing that delivery system.

Costa and Kallick suggest their own outcomes or goals that should drive the system. Their ideas for new goals to prepare students for the next century include the following:

- Capacity for continued learning,
- Knowing how to behave when answers to problems are not immediately apparent,
- Cooperativeness and team building,
- Precise communications in a variety of modes,
- Appreciation of disparate value systems,
- Problem solving that requires creativity and ingenuity,
- Enjoyment of resolving ambiguous, discrepant, or paradoxical situations,
- Organization of an overabundance of technologically produced information,
- Pride in a well-crafted product,
- High self-esteem, and
- Personal commitment to larger organizational and global values (Costa & Kallick, 1992, p. 275).

PAUSE

One important aspect of outcome-based education is the realization that not all students learn in the same way and at the same rate.

The methods of assessment must align with the new goals and measure whether or not students have achieved them. "We cannot employ product-oriented assessment techniques to assess the achievement of these new, process-oriented educational outcomes" (Costa & Kallick, 1992, p. 276).

Fogarty reminds us that the most significant outcome of all is "transfer of learning." Transfer of learning means the use in a new context of something learned in an earlier context. Yet research shows that most knowledge is inert or passive. The punctuation rules may be memorized for the multiple-choice test on Friday, but they are quickly forgotten when a student has to use them to write an essay on Monday. Inert knowledge does not contribute much to the cognitive ability of the learner. "One of the goals of teaching for transfer is teaching for active rather than inert knowledge" (Fogarty, 1992b, p. 349). If students cannot apply what they have learned to real-life situations, then true learning has not taken place.

Developing Thoughtful Outcomes

Educators across the country are trying to practice Costa's idea of "selective abandonment" with their curriculum by eliminating emphasis on discrete bits of factual information and concentrating instead on the significant exit outcomes they want students to demonstrate at the end of a lesson, day, unit, semester, or year. They are determining the exit outcomes they want all students to achieve *first* and then they "design back" and make sure that all the lessons relate to the exit outcome. Lessons in the restructured school reinforce what is really important for students to learn, not just for a test—but for a lifetime.

The following eleven exit outcomes were developed by District 214 in Arlington Heights, Illinois. They reflect the skills students need to demonstrate successfully before they graduate:

1. Ability to communicate (in reading, writing, speaking, listening, and numeracy skills)
2. Facility in social interaction
3. Analytical capabilities
4. Problem-solving skills
5. Skill in making value judgments and decisions
6. Skill in creative expression and in responding to the creative work of others
7. Civic responsibility

PAUSE

The methods of assessment must align with the new goals and measure whether or not students have achieved them.

8. Responsible participation in a global environment
9. Skill in developing and maintaining wellness
10. Skill in using technology as a tool for learning
11. Skill in life and career planning

(Fitzpatrick, 1991, pp. 18–19)

In addition to the broader general learner outcomes, many school systems like District 214 have also developed program outcomes. The program outcomes address the academic areas of English, mathematics, science, social studies, fine arts, physical education and health, foreign language, and practical arts as well as student services and student activities. The course outcomes relate to the outcomes for a specific course like American literature, geometry, biology, American history, or French 1.

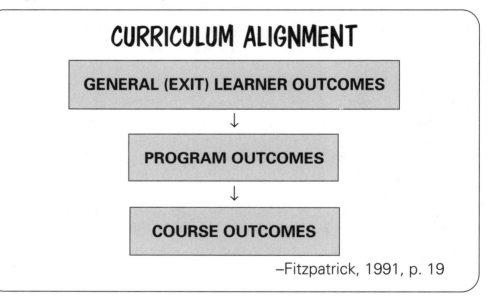

CURRICULUM ALIGNMENT

GENERAL (EXIT) LEARNER OUTCOMES

↓

PROGRAM OUTCOMES

↓

COURSE OUTCOMES

–Fitzpatrick, 1991, p. 19

PAUSE

Critical to determining whether or not students have achieved the desired outcome is to develop indicators to use as evidence.

Critical to determining whether or not students have achieved the desired outcome is to develop indicators to use as evidence. These specific indicators will show whether or not the student has made progress in his or her performance to achieve the outcome. For example, members of District 214 wanted their students to develop analytical capabilities as one of their general learner outcomes. They asked what would they accept as evidence that students had achieved that outcome, and came up with these four analytic capabilities:

• The student employs observation skills to acquire useful knowledge and information and classifies and organizes information;

- The student draws and supports inferences;
- The student describes and defines relationships such as cause/effect and comparison/contrast;
- The student integrates and applies skills in observation, classification, organization, inference, and in the definition of relationships in a variety of situations.

(Fitzpatrick, 1991, p. 19)

Indicators describe specific behaviors or demonstrations that are more concrete and measurable than broad outcomes. Teachers need to ask themselves, "What does problem solving look like or sound like?" if they are going to be able to recognize it when it happens. By listing indicators under each outcome, teachers and students will be able to know what specific things students say and do to demonstrate they have, in fact, achieved the outcome. It is essential to establish the indicators for each outcome if the assessment process is going to be meaningful. It is also important that students are aware of the outcomes and indicators and also have some input into creating them if they are to become active participants in the self-assessment process.

Thoughtful Outcomes and Assessment

The first question Tyler advised educators to ask before they devised their curriculum was, "What educational purposes should the school seek to attain?" Whether they are labeled "purposes," "goals," "demonstrations of learning," or "outcomes," it is essential that establishing the end result of education is critical. Emphasis should be placed on the learners, the products they produce, and the processes they use. Knowledge of content for the sake of knowledge alone is no longer a priority.

School personnel may have to redesign their whole curriculum, de-emphasize curriculum guides and textbooks in favor of resource-based instruction, and "selectively abandon" the overwhelming quantity of material to be "covered." Instead they need to emphasize the "quality of the experience." Covering fewer things well will be more meaningful than covering many things superficially, since students will retain what they actually experience.

Tyler's second fundamental question for curriculum development is, "What educational experiences can be provided that are likely to attain these purposes?" These experiences include cooperative learning, integrated curricula, higher-order thinking, problem-based

PAUSE

Knowledge of content for the sake of knowledge alone is no longer a priority.

PAUSE

Establishing thoughtful outcomes is critical to implementing authentic assessment.

learning, multiple intelligences, whole language, and a number of other learning experiences. How these experiences are organized to meet the needs of the learners is Tyler's third question for curriculum development. "How can we determine whether these purposes are being attained?" is the fourth question. If any of the pieces are missing, the curriculum will not be complete. The sandwich can be used as a metaphor to describe the other three critical components of learning. A person builds a sandwich by starting with the bottom piece of bread. One needs the solid foundation or thoughtful outcomes on which to build. The filling is the "meat" of the curriculum because without the meaningful content and effective learning experiences the sandwich would be dry, tasteless, and boring. Cooperative learning, problem-based learning, whole language, and integrated curricula are just some of the "meat" of the curriculum.

Once the first two layers are in place, the last layer, authentic assessment, completes the sandwich. The final piece answers Tyler's fourth question by finding out if all the goals have been attained. If any part of the sandwich is missing, it is still edible, but it's comparable to a school experience for millions of young people that Glasser calls "unsatisfying." It lacks flavor, wholeness, and customer satisfaction. Why leave parts out when the whole sandwich provides variety, sustenance, and, most importantly, lifelong learning.

FOOD FOR THOUGHT

AUTHENTIC ASSESSMENT

Cooperative Learning
Meaningful Content   Whole Language   Resource-Based Learning
Integrated Curricula   Problem-Based Learning

THOUGHTFUL LEARNER OUTCOMES

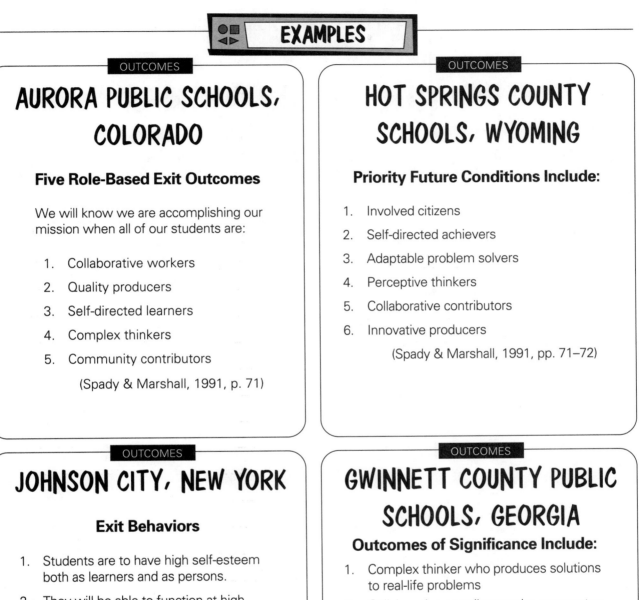

EXAMPLES

OUTCOMES

AURORA PUBLIC SCHOOLS, COLORADO

Five Role-Based Exit Outcomes

We will know we are accomplishing our mission when all of our students are:

1. Collaborative workers
2. Quality producers
3. Self-directed learners
4. Complex thinkers
5. Community contributors

(Spady & Marshall, 1991, p. 71)

OUTCOMES

HOT SPRINGS COUNTY SCHOOLS, WYOMING

Priority Future Conditions Include:

1. Involved citizens
2. Self-directed achievers
3. Adaptable problem solvers
4. Perceptive thinkers
5. Collaborative contributors
6. Innovative producers

(Spady & Marshall, 1991, pp. 71–72)

OUTCOMES

JOHNSON CITY, NEW YORK

Exit Behaviors

1. Students are to have high self-esteem both as learners and as persons.
2. They will be able to function at high cognitive levels, not just at the lower levels expected on standardized tests.
3. They will be good problem solvers, communicators, and decision makers; will be competent in group processes; and will be accountable for their own behavior.
4. They will be self-directed learners.
5. They will have concern for others.

(Vickery, 1988, pp. 52–53)

OUTCOMES

GWINNETT COUNTY PUBLIC SCHOOLS, GEORGIA

Outcomes of Significance Include:

1. Complex thinker who produces solutions to real-life problems
2. Collaborative contributor who cooperates effectively
3. Innovative producer who creates quality ideas, solutions, or products
4. Self-directed achiever who develops self-respect
5. Involved citizen who accepts responsibility for contributing time and talent
6. Effective communicator who informs, expresses self, and persuades

(excerpted from Gwinnett County Public Schools Outcomes Statement)

IRISkyLight

THOUGHTFUL OUTCOMES

Develop five thoughtful learner outcomes you would like your students to demonstrate at the end of a unit, semester, or year.

Outcome #1 _____

_____

_____

_____

Outcome #2 _____

_____

_____

_____

Outcome #3 _____

_____

_____

_____

Outcome #4 _____

_____

_____

_____

Outcome #5 _____

_____

_____

_____

IRI SkyLight

INDICATORS

Write indicators for three of the outcomes you developed on the previous page. Indicators provide specific behaviors that demonstrate the student has achieved the outcome.

Example: Outcome: Students will become effective communicators.

Indicators: Students will:
- Write to communicate ideas and feelings.
- Write to persuade, entertain, and communicate technical information.
- Speak to inform, persuade, and entertain.
- Listen and respond to others empathetically.

Outcome #1: _____
  Indicators: Students will:
- _____
- _____
- _____
- _____

Outcome #2: _____
  Indicators: Students will:
- _____
- _____
- _____
- _____

Outcome #3: _____
  Indicators: Students will:
- _____
- _____
- _____
- _____

IRISkyLight

THOUGHTFUL OUTCOMES
REFLECTION PAGE

RECORD

1. Examine the course outline, syllabus, or curriculum guide for your class or one course you teach. Practice "selective abandonment" by eliminating those lessons or units that do not relate to the outcomes you developed and listing the lessons that do contribute to the thoughtful outcomes.

    CONTENT: _____

What can you eliminate?	What should you keep?

2. Reflect on how you feel about abandoning that special lesson or unit. How can you do a better job with the things you have left? Compare your list with that of a colleague who teaches the same material to see if you both agree on what should stay and what should go. Discuss your decisions.

IRI SkyLight

STANDARDIZED TESTS

CHAPTER 2

"Academic achievement can be
assessed in many ways, but when the
public and policymakers seek
evidence of school quality, they
usually look to standardized tests.
These tests have a potent influence
on education policy and on public
perceptions of schools."

-Archbald & Newmann, 1988, p. 52

WHAT ARE STANDARDIZED TESTS?

Standardized tests are administered and scored under conditions uniform to all students. Although the public associates standardized tests with the multiple-choice format, standardization is really a generic concept that can apply to any testing format. In order to make test scores comparable, test takers need to have equal chances to demonstrate what they know. "A standardized test score is an accurate measure of a student's test-taking ability *relative to the norming population*" (Archbald & Newmann, 1988, p. 54). "The word 'standardized' is used to designate the fact that the tests are administered, scored, and interpreted in a standard way and that the tests are accompanied by 'norms.' Norms are records of the performances made by groups of individuals who have previously taken the test. They are used as a means of determining how the score of any individual who takes the test compares with scores made by other persons" (Wandt & Brown, 1957, p. 74). Standardized tests are usually considered to be more objective, accurate, and easily comparable than teacher-made tests and assessments.

Wiggins reminds us that standardized testing evolved and proliferated because the school transcript became untrustworthy. "An 'A' in 'English' means only that some adult thought the student's work was excellent. Compared to what or whom? As determined by what criteria? In reference to what specific subject matter?" (Wiggins, 1989, p. 122). Students can receive a high school diploma by putting in "seat time," but does anyone really know what they can do?

The College Entrance Examination Board introduced the Scholastic Aptitude Test (SAT) in 1926 as an efficient and economical instrument to help college offices select the most promising students from among the increasing number of applicants. Many colleges found that the results of the aptitude tests constituted a better predictor of college achievement than high school grades (Schudson, 1972). With the introduction of the SAT, aptitude tests were on their way to becoming a major factor in educational decisions.

Archbald and Newmann (1988) note that even though academic achievement can be assessed in a wide variety of ways, the public and policymakers generally measure the quality of schools by standardized test scores. Published test scores, therefore, have become

PAUSE

"An 'A' in 'English' means only that some adult thought the student's work was excellent. Compared to what or whom?"

-Wiggins, 1989, p. 122

the yardsticks by which education is measured. Members of the Education Commission of the States conducted 650 hours of interviews and observations with administrators and teachers and found that "almost everyone [they] talked to is determining educational success or progress on the basis of scores on commercial standardized norm-referenced tests" (Brown, 1989, p. 113).

Some people feel that in the United States today, standardized testing is running amok. "Newspapers rank schools and districts by their test scores. Real estate agents use test scores to identify the 'best' schools as selling points for expensive housing. Superintendents can be fired for low scores, and teachers can receive merit pay for high scores. Superintendents exhort principals and principals admonish teachers to raise test scores—rather than to increase learning" (Shepard, 1989, p. 4).

Aptitude tests are instruments that estimate aspects of an individual's developed abilities to attain knowledge acquired both in and out of school. Achievement tests are intended to estimate what a student knows and can do in a specific subject such as English or social studies based on what he or she has studied in school. Both tests are designed to estimate aspects of an individual's developed abilities.

Student performance on standardized tests is interpreted in two ways. *Norm-referenced tests* are designed to test a student's performance as it compares to that of other students. For example, "Max typed faster than eighty percent of his classmates did."

Criterion-referenced tests, on the other hand, are designed to compare a student's test performance to learning tasks or skill levels. For example, "Max typed thirty words per minute without mistakes." A criterion-referenced test, therefore, draws its meaning from the domain of behaviors the test is designed to represent.

Two key points in evaluating standardized tests are validity and reliability. Validity is the degree to which a measurement technique obtains the kind of evidence which its user intends to collect. Reliability is the degree to which a measurement technique obtains accurate and consistent evidence (Wandt & Brown, 1957).

PAUSE

Aptitude tests are instruments that estimate aspects of an individual's developed abilities to attain knowledge acquired both in and out of school.

WHY CHALLENGE STANDARDIZED TESTS?

Emphasis on Recall and Prior Knowledge

Even though standardized tests purport to measure the cognitive abilities required for academic and nonacademic tasks, Marzano and Costa (1988) found that there have been few research attempts to validate the assumption that they do, in fact, measure cognitive skills. One study, however, conducted by the Midcontinent Regional Educational Laboratory analyzed 6,942 items from the Stanford Achievement batteries and the California Test of Basic Skills to identify the general cognitive abilities tested and study their relationships to student performance (Marzano & Jesse, in Marzano & Costa, 1988, p. 66).

The results of the analysis showed the following two major findings: "(1) the test items included only nine of the twenty-two general cognitive operations, and (2) the general cognitive operations required to answer the questions had very little to do with student achievement on those tests" (Marzano & Costa, 1988, p. 67).

These findings imply that "standardized tests in their present form [1988] are primarily measures of factual or declarative information" and that "school districts that wish to perform well on standardized tests would do better to teach the facts contained in standardized tests rather than teach generic thinking skills" (Marzano & Costa, 1988, p. 70).

Marzano and Costa (1988) advocate restructuring standardized tests to emphasize more complex process knowledge in lieu of factual or declarative knowledge. Instead of the single-answer, multiple-choice tests, multiple answers should be permitted. They also recommend using more ongoing assessments by teachers in the classroom to observe, interact, document, and interpret cognitive operations.

The introduction of more qualitative assessment techniques would require a shift from paper-and-pencil tests to a broader view of assessment as a combination of both qualitative and quantitative techniques.

PAUSE

[▐▐]

"School districts that wish to perform well on standardized tests would do better to teach the facts contained in standardized tests rather than teach generic thinking skills."

-Marzano & Costa, 1988, p. 70

Advantages of Standardized Tests

Standardized tests were never intended to be the key component of student evaluation. They were intended to be a valuable ingredient that would combine with many other assessments to create a more accurate picture of a student's educational profile.

Standardized tests offer the following advantages:
1. Standardized test scores allow simple comparisons between students, schools, districts, states, and nations.
2. They are easily administered.
3. [They] take little time away from instruction, and
4. With a long history of use by psychometricians and major institutions, they carry scientific credibility (Archbald & Newmann, 1988, p. 52).

Even though standardized tests should play only a minor part in student evaluation, they have become in many situations the major component.

PAUSE

Standardized tests were never intended to be the key component of student evaluation.

Disadvantages of Standardized Tests

Standardized tests of knowledge in specific content areas such as foreign language, literature, and science may not have some of the following disadvantages, but tests of general achievement and ability usually do. Unfortunately, most secondary schools rely on the tests of general achievement and ability to measure students' verbal, numerical, and analytical abilities.

Archbald and Newmann list three major disadvantages of using standardized tests to measure general achievement and ability:

1. The difficulty of gaining useful information due to the way all standardized tests are constructed and scored
2. Special problems of general achievement and ability tests due to their insensitivity to curriculum in specific subject areas and their lack of predictive relationship to more authentic forms of achievement
3. The tendency of items in all standardized tests (even those of specific subject areas) to neglect the assessment of depth of understanding, integration of knowledge, and production of discourse (Archbald & Newmann, 1988, p. 53).

Limitations

Shepard (1989) offers other limitations of standardized tests. She argues that large-scale testing programs are limited by both political and practical considerations that compromise their ability to measure significant learning outcomes.

- **The negotiation of content.** Most tests go through a consensus-building process that limits the depth of content coverage. Test publishers ensure that test objectives are matched to widely used textbooks that are homogenized by the consensus-building model to ensure wide market appeal.
- **The narrowing of content.** Test construction emphasizes basic skills. Since many teachers tend to "teach to the test," basic skills are emphasized at the expense of higher-order thinking skills. Minimum competency tests are even narrower than standardized tests of basic skills.
- **Multiple-choice formats.** Test developers rely heavily on multiple-choice formats on tests because of the time and money involved. This format is much cheaper and faster to grade. Tasks which would require students to produce or explain a correct answer are not cost effective.

"Although multiple-choice questions can elicit important conceptual distinctions from students, tests composed entirely of such items do not measure a respondent's ability to organize relevant information and present a coherent argument" (Shepard, 1989, p. 5).

The Impact of Standardized Tests

Despite the disadvantages and limitations of many standardized tests, educators across the country are using the results of standardized tests to track or place students, to promote students, to accept students into classes, programs, special schools, or colleges, to apply for federal funds, and to determine honors, awards, and scholarships. Yet, research shows that people have mixed feelings about the impact standardized tests have on instruction and evaluation.

Brown and the Education Commission of the States gathered 650 hours' worth of interview and observational information and formulated the following generalizations:

1. Schools that are not in the public doghouse or under tight court monitoring do testing routinely, make little use of the

PAUSE

"**Schools that are not in the public doghouse or under tight court monitoring do their testing routinely, make little use of the results, and go about their business.**"
-Brown, 1989, p. 113

results, and go about their business.

2. Schools under public scrutiny…encourage much more teaching to the test and make much more out of declines or increases in scores.

3. Experienced, confident teachers pay little attention to externally imposed tests.

4. New teachers, however, and underprepared or insecure or embattled teachers, are more likely to teach to the tests, even if they believe the tests are poor indicators of student learning.

5. Most people…believe that commercial standardized tests are valid indicators of student and school achievement.

6. Although many researchers and even testing experts see serious limitations to these tests and caution users constantly about misuse or misinterpretation, school people seldom showed awareness or concern about these matters.

7. When we asked whether the tests adequately addressed higher-order thinking skills or performances (they do not), they either didn't know, didn't care, or believed the test manufacturer had dealt with that problem.

(Brown, 1989, p. 113)

HOW CAN STANDARDIZED TESTS CHANGE?

Standardized tests, along with most other types of teacher-made tests, must change in order to assess the significant learning outcomes that are important for all students to learn. "The prevailing teaching and testing technology rests on the assumption that knowledge is objective and can be drilled into passive 'blank-slate' brains, then paraded out on cue. This may apply to some kinds of knowledge—for instance, multiplication tables. But most knowledge is socially and personally derived; we are creating it all the time through social interaction, and its nature and uses constantly shift" (Brown, 1989, p. 114).

Haney (in Marzano & Costa, 1988) says a shift away from the paper-and-pencil tests to an array of qualitative techniques would not violate the original intent of standardized tests. According to Haney,

PAUSE

"The prevailing teaching and testing technology rests on the assumption that knowledge is objective and can be drilled into passive 'blank-slate' brains, then paraded out on cue."

-Brown, 1989, p. 114

21

standardized tests were originally just one of the many pieces of data used to assess student competence. Since the introduction of the standardized test, however, it has gradually come to be the *major* criterion of performance and ability. Instead of being just one segment of a student's video portfolio, it has become, in some cases, the whole video.

PAUSE

"There is no reason to do away entirely with standardized tests that do not promote cheating. The task is to keep them from dominating school affairs to such a degree that they distort curriculum and hold back efforts to make schools more thoughtful places."
-Brown, 1989, p. 115

According to Pipho, "It appears that state testing programs are in for some kind of change. States such as California and Kentucky, and organizations such as the National Governors' Association, are leading the way in the shake-up of the industry" (Burke, 1992a, p. 31).

Many states and consortiums that used to administer traditional norm-referenced tests are now developing new programs of performance-based assessment. Also, many new standardized tests at the state and the national level are including items with multiple answers and open-ended questions as well as performance-based assessments such as writing, speaking, and problem solving.

If more states and testing agencies do, indeed, revise standardized tests to reflect actual performances, higher-order thinking skills, and concrete learning beyond filling in bubbles, these tests can be a valuable tool. Standardized tests can be used diagnostically to find out a student's learning deficiency or a teacher's teaching deficiency. They can also be used to determine levels of achievement of individuals or groups, to gauge a student's development, and to help judge the quality of the curriculum.

If standardized tests can be revised to measure thoughtful outcomes, they should play an important role in a student's portfolio. It would be ludicrous to cut an integral shot in the video just because it is a little out of focus. Test makers just need to do some fine tuning to adjust to the way students learn—not to how they take tests!

"There is no reason to do away entirely with standardized tests that do not promote cheating (e.g., everyone's being 'above average'). The task is to keep them from dominating school affairs to such a degree that they distort curriculum and hold back efforts to make schools more thoughtful places" (Brown, 1989, p. 115).

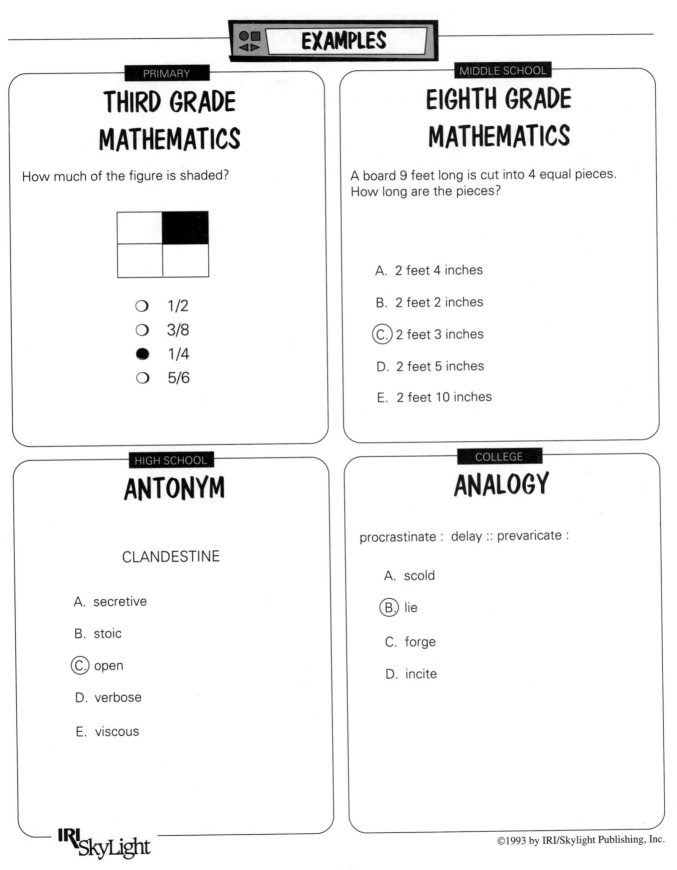

EXAMPLES

PRIMARY

THIRD GRADE MATHEMATICS

How much of the figure is shaded?

- ○ 1/2
- ○ 3/8
- ● 1/4
- ○ 5/6

MIDDLE SCHOOL

EIGHTH GRADE MATHEMATICS

A board 9 feet long is cut into 4 equal pieces. How long are the pieces?

- A. 2 feet 4 inches
- B. 2 feet 2 inches
- C. 2 feet 3 inches
- D. 2 feet 5 inches
- E. 2 feet 10 inches

HIGH SCHOOL

ANTONYM

CLANDESTINE

- A. secretive
- B. stoic
- C. open
- D. verbose
- E. viscous

COLLEGE

ANALOGY

procrastinate : delay :: prevaricate :

- A. scold
- B. lie
- C. forge
- D. incite

IRI SkyLight

ON YOUR OWN

STANDARDIZED TESTS

1. Select one standardized test that either you or your students have taken. Analyze some of the test questions and label them according to the following categories:

   a. prior knowledge needed

   b. recall question

   c. higher-order thinking question

   d. ambiguous question

   e. more than one answer seems correct

   f. culturally biased

   g. other

2. Comment on your findings.

   _____

   _____

   _____

   _____

   _____

   _____

   _____

   _____

   _____

   _____

IRI SkyLight

©1993 by IRI/Skylight Publishing, Inc.

STANDARDIZED TEST ITEMS

Write sample test items that would be appropriate for your students.

Example:

Analogy: Procrastinate is to Delay as Prevaricate is to
  a) chew   c) lie
  b) scold   d) avoid

Sentence Completion _____

_____

_____

_____

_____

Antonym _____

_____

_____

_____

_____

Synonym _____

_____

_____

_____

_____

Mathematics Problem _____

_____

_____

_____

_____

©1993 by IRI/Skylight Publishing, Inc.

STANDARDIZED TESTS
REFLECTION PAGE

RECORD

1. Reflect on one standardized test you administered to your students. What do you remember about that test and their reactions to it?

_____

_____

_____

_____

_____

_____

_____

_____

2. Can you remember a standardized test you took? Explain how you felt.

_____

_____

_____

_____

3. How do you feel about the way standardized tests are used in your school? Could you offer any suggestions for changes?

_____

_____

_____

_____

TEACHER-MADE TESTS

22. QUESTION

_____
_____
_____
_____
_____

ANSWER

_____
_____
_____
_____

CHAPTER **3**

"Since we have rarely inquired into
the quality of teacher-developed tests,
offered training in classroom
assessment, or included classroom
assessment in the principal's
leadership role, we simply do not
know how well teachers measure
student achievement or how to help
them if they need help."

-Stiggins, 1985, p. 72

WHAT ARE TEACHER-MADE TESTS?

Teacher-made tests are written or oral assessments that are not commercially produced or standardized. In other words, a test a teacher designs specifically for his or her students. "Testing" refers to any kind of school activity that results in some type of mark or comment being entered in a checklist, grade book, or anecdotal record. The term "test," however, refers to a more structured oral or written evaluation of student achievement. Examinations are tests that are school scheduled, tend to cover more of the curriculum, and count more than other forms of evaluation (Board of Education for the City of Etobicoke, 1987).

The word "test" has negative connotations for many students, who equate the word with "fear," "sickness," "embarrassment," and, of course, "failure." For too many years students have been penalized, not because they did not understand the material, but because they could not understand the test. If teachers teach what is important, they must also test what is important. If teacher-made tests contain important outcomes students *should* know, then teachers *should* teach to the test.

Teacher-made tests can be important parts of the teaching and learning process if they are integrated into daily classroom teaching and are constructed to be part of the learning process—not just the culminating event. They allow students to see their own progress and allow teachers to make adjustments to their instruction on a daily basis. "But one of the most serious problems of evaluation is the fact that a primary means of assessment—the test itself—is often severely flawed or misused" (Hills, 1991, p. 541).

Constructing a good teacher-made test is very time consuming and difficult; moreover, it is hard to understand why something so essential to the learning process should be virtually ignored in teacher preservice or inservice training. Veteran teachers cannot believe that many of them have relied on commercially made tests in workbooks or on their own inadequate teacher-made tests for most of their evaluations. They have often neglected addressing this aspect of teaching because they were not trained to use assessment and no one at the school focused on one of the most essential components of learning—assessment.

PAUSE

Teacher-made tests can be important parts of the teaching and learning process if they are integrated into daily classroom teaching.

28

One of the problems with teacher-made tests is their emphasis on lower-level thinking. A study conducted by the Cleveland Public Schools (Fleming & Chambers, 1983, as cited in Stiggins, 1985) examined over 300 teacher-made, paper-and-pencil tests. The results of the study found that teachers appeared to need training in how to do the following:

1. plan and write longer tests;
2. write unambiguous paper-and-pencil test items; and
3. measure skills beyond recall of facts
    (Stiggins, 1985, p. 72).

The research also found that teachers often overlooked quality control factors like establishing written criteria for performances or planning scoring procedures in advance. Wiggins notes that "course-specific tests also have glaring weaknesses, not only because they are often too low level and content heavy. They are rarely designed to be authentic tests of intellectual ability; as with standardized tests, teacher-designed finals are usually intended to be quickly read and scored" (Wiggins, 1989, p. 123).

Teacher-made tests do not carry the same importance as standardized tests in public relations between the school and the community. Even though many of them have the same objective-style format that allows for easy comparisons, they are not seen as reliable and valid. Teacher-made tests are suspect because they differ greatly from class to class and their quality is often questioned. Just like standardized tests which have a standard error of measurement associated with them, so too do teacher-made tests carry an error factor. Since administrators devote so much time and energy coordinating and monitoring standardized tests, they do not have the time or, in many cases, the experience to help teachers construct better teacher-made tests (Stiggins, 1985).

Since so few states or colleges of education require teachers to take courses in assessment, many teachers enter the classroom with very little training in how to create meaningful tests. They either remember the types of tests they took as students or they model the tests on ones provided by their fellow teachers or in workbooks. Unfortunately, most of the tests teachers took as students were multiple-choice, recall tests that covered a great deal of content with very little emphasis on higher-order thinking. Teachers have had very little practice constructing problem-solving situations on tests to measure the application of skills.

PAUSE

Teacher-made tests are suspect because they differ greatly from class to class and their quality is often questioned.

Stiggins (1985) recommends that resources be allocated to provide technical assistance to teachers in the development and use of classroom assessments. Teachers need help designing and constructing better tests, scoring them, and analyzing the results. They also should be encouraged to experiment with better ways to measure important outcomes.

"Such personalized, continuous training could have a very positive impact on instruction—not only because teachers would develop or improve testing skills, but also because the provision of specialized training would say to teachers clearly and unequivocally that their assessment insights and judgments are valued and respected" (Stiggins, 1985, p. 74).

PAUSE

Teacher-made tests allow teachers to make decisions that keep instruction moving.

WHY DO WE NEED BETTER TEACHER-MADE TESTS?

Even though parents and the media value published test scores, most teachers do not rely on standardized tests to tell them what their students know and don't know. Standardized tests occur so infrequently that one aggregate score is not very helpful in determining future instructional goals. Teacher-made tests, however, allow teachers to make decisions that keep instruction moving. Teachers can make changes immediately to meet the needs of their students. "They [teachers] rely most heavily on assessments provided as part of instructional materials and assessments they design and construct themselves—and very little on standardized tests or test scores" (Stiggins, 1985, p. 69).

The key to teacher-made tests is to make them a part of assessment—not separate from it. Tests should be instructional and ongoing. Rather than being "after-the-fact" to find out what students did *not learn*, they should be more "during-the-fact" to see what they still *need to learn* and to determine different instructional methods to ensure success.

Teachers also need to make adjustments in their tests for the various learning styles, multiple intelligences, and learning problems of the students in their classes. It would be impossible to address every student's need on every test, but efforts should be made to construct tests that motivate, provide choices, and make allowances for individual differences.

Learning Modalities

Teachers need to construct better tests to adjust for students' learning modalities and to make modifications for at-risk students. Frender (1990) defines learning modalities as ways of using sensory information to learn. Three of the five senses are primarily used in learning, storing, and recalling information. Because students learn from and communicate best with someone who shares their dominant modality, it is important for teachers to know the characteristics of their students so that they can at least alter their instructional styles and tests to match the learning styles of all the students.

Frender has identified many characteristics of the three styles of learning. The following represent the characteristics that could most likely influence students' test-taking skills.

PAUSE

Teachers need to construct better tests to adjust for students' learning modalities and to make modifications for at-risk students.

TYPES OF LEARNERS

VISUAL LEARNERS	AUDITORY LEARNERS	KINESTHETIC LEARNERS
mind sometimes strays during verbal activities	talks to self	in motion most of the time
organized in approach to tasks	easily distracted	reading is not a priority
likes to read	has difficulty with written directions	poor speller
usually a good speller	likes to be read to	likes to solve problems by physically walking through them
memorizes by seeing graphics and pictures	memorizes by steps in a sequence	enjoys handling objects
finds verbal instructions difficult	enjoys listening activities	enjoys doing activities

(Adapted from Frender, 1990, p. 25)

Modifications for Students with Special Needs

With the movement toward inclusive classrooms, teachers need to be able to meet the needs of students with learning disabilities, behavior exceptionalities, physical exceptionalities, and intellectual exceptionalities. In addition, as society becomes a "salad bowl" of many ethnic groups, teacher-made tests must allow opportunities for non-English speaking students to succeed. Many schools have now detracked, thereby merging all levels of students (gifted, average, remedial) into one inclusive class. It would be impossible to use one objective test to measure the growth and development of all students. Authentic tests can celebrate diversity by allowing students a wide variety of ways to demonstrate what they know and what they can do.

Teacher-made tests can be constructed to meet the needs of all students by providing many opportunities to measure what students can do instead of just measuring their ability to read, write, and take tests.

The following modifications can be made to help ensure success on tests for all students, especially those with special needs who are most at risk of failing tests:

1. Read instructions orally.
2. Rephrase oral instructions if needed.
3. Ask students to repeat directions to make sure they understand.
4. Monitor carefully to make sure all students understand directions for test.
5. Provide alternative evaluations—oral testing, use of tapes, test given in another room, dictation.
6. Make sure instructions are easily understood.
7. Give examples of each type of question (oral and written).
8. Leave enough space for answers.
9. Use visual demonstrations or examples.
10. Use white paper.
11. Do not crowd or clutter the test.
12. Give choices.
13. Go from concrete to abstract.
14. Don't deduct for spelling or grammar on tests.
15. Use some take-home tests.

PAUSE

Authentic tests can celebrate diversity by allowing students a wide variety of ways to demonstrate what they know and what they can do.

16. Provide manipulative experiences whenever possible.
17. Allow students to use notes and textbooks during some tests.
18. Allow students to write down key math or science formulas (students are not penalized for poor memory).
19. Include visuals like graphic organizers on tests.
20. Provide immediate feedback on all tests.
21. Allow students to correct mistakes and/or to retake tests to improve scores and understand what they didn't understand on the first test.

(Adapted from Board of Education for the City of Etobicoke, 1987, pp. 204–214)

HOW CAN WE CONSTRUCT BETTER TEACHER-MADE TESTS?

Most teachers will not have time to rewrite all their tests to conform to specific guidelines. However, it is important to construct some tests that incorporate many of the ideas in this chapter. If, as Wiggins suggests, "we should teach to the authentic test," students should also be brought into the test-making process. They can help construct meaningful tests based on thoughtful outcomes. Brown recommends that teachers draw students into the development of tests. He says nothing helps a person master a subject better than having to ask and debate fundamental questions about what is most important about that subject and how someone could tell if he or she has mastered it. "Students of all ages who create some of their own examinations are forced to reflect on what they have studied and make judgments about it" (Brown, 1989, p. 115).

The following guidelines may help in the construction of better teacher-made tests.

Guidelines for Teacher-Made Tests

1. Make sure the test is correlated to course objectives or learning outcomes.
2. Give clear directions for each section of the test.
3. Arrange the questions from simple to complex.

PAUSE

"Students of all ages who create some of their own examinations are forced to reflect on what they have studied and make judgments about it."
-Brown, 1989, p. 115

PAUSE

⏸

Essays, graphic organizers, oral performances, and artistic presentations measure meaningful outcomes and can all be included on teacher-made tests.

4. Give point values for each section (e.g., true/false [2 points each])
5. Vary the question types (true/false, fill-in-the-blank, multiple choice, essay, matching).
6. Group question types together.
7. Type or print clearly. (Leave space between questions to facilitate easy reading and writing.)
8. Make sure appropriate reading level is used.
9. Include a variety of visual, oral, and kinesthetic tasks.
10. Make allowances for students with special needs.
11. Give students some choice in the questions they select (e.g., a choice of graphic organizers or essay questions).
12. Vary levels of questions by using the three-story intellect verbs (p. 38) to cover gathering, processing, and application questions.
13. Provide a grading scale so students know what score constitutes a certain grade (e.g., 93–100 = A; 85–92 = B; 75–84 = C; 70–74 = D; Below 70 = Not Yet!).
14. Give sufficient time for all students to finish. (The teacher should be able to work through the test in one-third to one-half the time given students.)

Question Types

One way teachers can construct better teacher-made tests is to consider the types of questions that should be included on a test. Obviously, it is important to select items that will measure whether or not the students have achieved the significant learning outcomes of the unit.

Essays, graphic organizers, oral performances, and artistic presentations measure meaningful outcomes and can all be included on teacher-made tests. Because of time constraints, however, many teachers choose to use objective-style questions. Objective-style questions have highly specific, predetermined answers that require a short response.

Objective-style questions include the following:

1. multiple choice
2. true-false
3. matching
4. short response

Even though objective-style questions can play a role in the assessment process, they, like standardized tests, must be put in the proper perspective.

"Evaluation should be a learning experience for both the student and the teacher. However, objective-style testing is frequently ineffective as a learning experience for either the student or the teacher because objective-style questions too often require only the recall of facts and do not allow the student to display thinking processes or the teacher to observe them" (Board of Education for the City of Etobicoke, 1987, p. 156).

A good evaluation program does not have to include objective-style tests; however, if it does, the questions should be well-constructed and the objective-style tests should be balanced by other authentic assessments.

Teachers should examine both the advantages and disadvantages of objective-style tests and then determine the role they will play in the evaluation process.

PAUSE

. . .objective-style tests should be balanced by other authentic assessments.

OBJECTIVE TYPES OF EVALUATION

A well-developed objective test:

ADVANTAGES	DISADVANTAGES
• can evaluate skills quickly and efficiently • can prevent students from "writing around" the answer • can prevent students' grades from being influenced by writing skills, spelling, grammar, and neatness • can be easily analyzed (item analysis) • prevents biased grading by teacher • can be used for diagnostic or pre-test purposes • can be given to large groups	• requires mostly recall of fact • will not allow students to demonstrate writing skills • often requires a disproportionate amount of reading (penalizes poor readers) • can be ambiguous and confusing (especially to younger students) • usually has a specific, predetermined answer • can be very time consuming to construct • promotes guessing • is often used year after year despite differing needs of students

(Adapted from the Board of Education for the City of Etobicoke, 1987, pp. 157–158)

Constructing Good Test Items

Entire education courses are devoted to helping teachers construct good test items. It would be impossible to describe the process in detail, but the following pages include a few short tips that might help.

Bellanca and Fogarty (1991) have created a graphic called the Three-Story Intellect to show what verbs teachers can use when they ask questions. First-story verbs like "count," "describe," and "match," ask students to gather or *recall* information. Second-story verbs like "reason," "compare," and "analyze" ask students to *process* information. And the third-story verbs like "evaluate," "imagine," and "speculate" ask students to *apply* information. A good teacher-made test includes verbs from all three stories of the intellect. Many teachers use this graphic as a guide when they ask questions in class and when they create teacher-made tests that encourage higher-order thinking.

PAUSE

A good teacher-made test includes verbs from all three stories of the intellect.

"Professor, what is this relic?"

"It's a primitive torture device used by teachers in the 20th century. They called it a Scantron machine."

Scores mult & T+F questions

TIPS FOR CONSTRUCTING QUESTION TYPES

True-False Items
- Avoid absolute words like "all," "never," and "always."
- Make sure items are clearly true or false rather than ambiguous.
- Limit true-false questions to 10.
- Consider asking students to make false questions true to encourage higher-order thinking.

Matching Items
- Limit list to between 5 and 15 items.
- Use homogeneous lists. (Don't mix names with dates.)
- Give clear instructions. (Write letter, number, etc.)
- Give more choices than there are questions.

Multiple-Choice Items
- State main idea in the core or stem of the question.
- Use reasonable incorrect choices. (Avoid ridiculous choices.)
- Make options the same length (nothing very long or very short).
- Include multiple correct answers (a and b, all of the above).

Completion Items
- Structure for a brief, specific answer for each item.
- Avoid passages lifted directly from text (emphasis on memorization).
- Use blanks of equal length.
- Avoid multiple blanks that sometimes make a sentence too confusing.

Essay Items
- Avoid all-encompassing questions ("Discuss" is ambiguous...tell all you know about a subject).
- Define criteria for evaluation.
- Define point value.
- Use some higher-order thinking verbs like "predict" or "compare and contrast" rather than all recall verbs like "list" and "name."

(Adapted from Board of Education for the City of Etobicoke, 1987, pp. 112–187.)

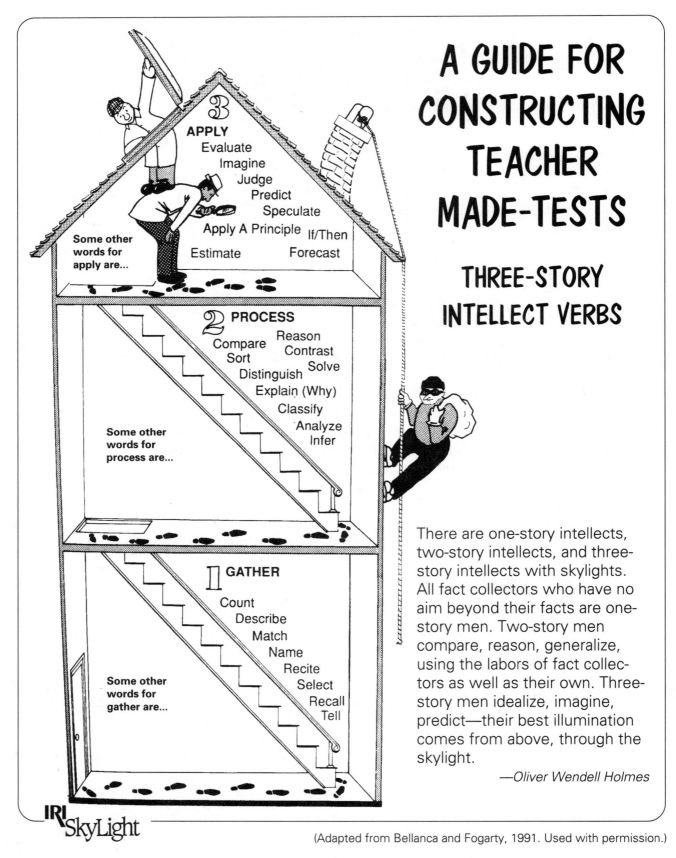

A GUIDE FOR CONSTRUCTING TEACHER MADE-TESTS

THREE-STORY INTELLECT VERBS

3 APPLY
Evaluate
Imagine
Judge
Predict
Speculate
Apply A Principle   If/Then
Estimate   Forecast

Some other words for apply are...

2 PROCESS
Compare   Reason
Sort   Contrast
Distinguish   Solve
Explain (Why)
Classify
Analyze
Infer

Some other words for process are...

1 GATHER
Count
Describe
Match
Name
Recite
Select
Recall
Tell

Some other words for gather are...

There are one-story intellects, two-story intellects, and three-story intellects with skylights. All fact collectors who have no aim beyond their facts are one-story men. Two-story men compare, reason, generalize, using the labors of fact collectors as well as their own. Three-story men idealize, imagine, predict—their best illumination comes from above, through the skylight.

—*Oliver Wendell Holmes*

IRI SkyLight

(Adapted from Bellanca and Fogarty, 1991. Used with permission.)

EXAMPLES

MATCHING QUESTIONS

SOCIAL STUDIES TEST ON SOUTHEASTERN UNITED STATES

Directions: (Three points each.) On the line to the left of Column A, write the letter of the phrase in Column B that best matches the word.

Column A

1. _I_ Tobacco
2. _B_ Cotton Gin
3. _G_ Plantation
4. _J_ Cash Crops
5. _A_ Crop Rotation
6. _C_ Tourist
7. _D_ Service Jobs
8. _F_ Cotton

Column B

A. Changing crops from one year to another.
B. Separated cotton seeds from cotton.
C. Someone who visits a place for pleasure.
D. Jobs that do things for other people.
E. People who lived in the Colonies
F. Once referred to as "White Gold."
G. Biggest farms in the Southeast.
H. Jobs that produce products.
I. First cash crop.
J. Crops grown to earn money.

(Courtesy of Nancy Minske, District #21, Wheeling, IL)

GRAPHIC ORGANIZER

HISTORY

Directions: Complete the mind map on the Middle Ages by filling in the main components in the big circles and the subpoints in the smaller circles. (1 point per circle)

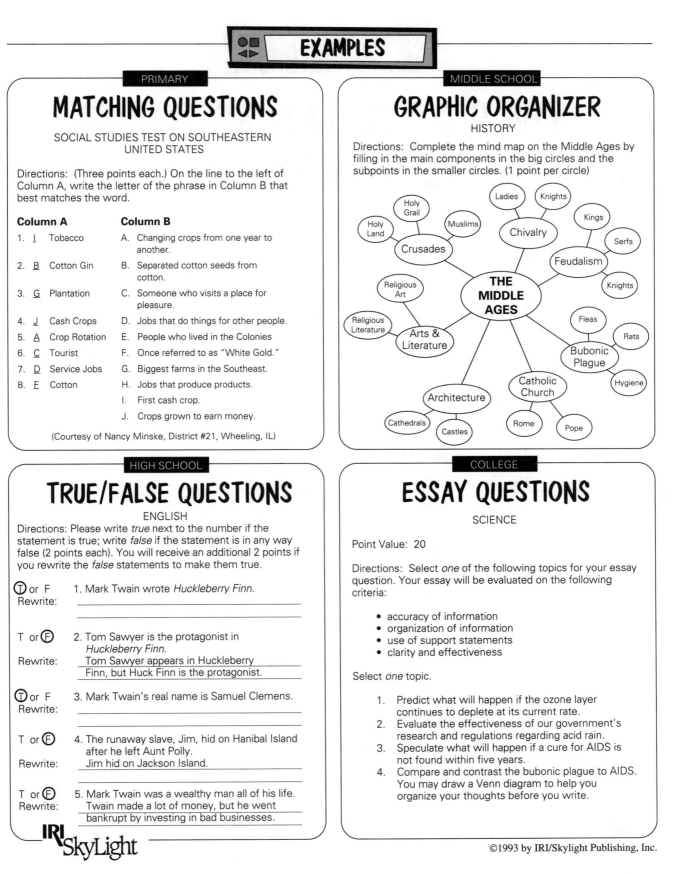

TRUE/FALSE QUESTIONS

ENGLISH

Directions: Please write *true* next to the number if the statement is true; write *false* if the statement is in any way false (2 points each). You will receive an additional 2 points if you rewrite the *false* statements to make them true.

Ⓣ or F   1. Mark Twain wrote *Huckleberry Finn*.
Rewrite: _____

T or Ⓕ   2. Tom Sawyer is the protagonist in *Huckleberry Finn*.
Rewrite: Tom Sawyer appears in Huckleberry Finn, but Huck Finn is the protagonist.

Ⓣ or F   3. Mark Twain's real name is Samuel Clemens.
Rewrite: _____

T or Ⓕ   4. The runaway slave, Jim, hid on Hanibal Island after he left Aunt Polly.
Rewrite: Jim hid on Jackson Island.

T or Ⓕ   5. Mark Twain was a wealthy man all of his life.
Rewrite: Twain made a lot of money, but he went bankrupt by investing in bad businesses.

ESSAY QUESTIONS

SCIENCE

Point Value: 20

Directions: Select *one* of the following topics for your essay question. Your essay will be evaluated on the following criteria:

- accuracy of information
- organization of information
- use of support statements
- clarity and effectiveness

Select *one* topic.

1. Predict what will happen if the ozone layer continues to deplete at its current rate.
2. Evaluate the effectiveness of our government's research and regulations regarding acid rain.
3. Speculate what will happen if a cure for AIDS is not found within five years.
4. Compare and contrast the bubonic plague to AIDS. You may draw a Venn diagram to help you organize your thoughts before you write.

THE BIG TEN TEACHER-MADE TEST CHECKLIST

Test: _____ Date: _____

Grade Level/Class: _____

1. ____I have listed my thoughtful outcomes on the test.

2. ____I have varied the question types to include ____ types.

3. ____I have given point values for each section.

4. ____I have arranged test items from simple to complex.

5. ____I have included tasks for the visual, auditory, and kinesthetic learners.

6. ____I have given students some choice of questions.

7. ____I have used all three levels of the Three-Story Intellect
verbs in my questions.

8. ____I have made allowances for students with special needs.

9. ____I have made sure that all students have time to finish the
test or have been provided with extra time if needed.

10. ____I have listed my grading scale on the test.

Signature: _____

IRI
SkyLight

ON YOUR OWN

THREE-STORY INTELLECT VERBS REVIEW

1. Analyze one of your own teacher-made tests. Classify the questions by marking them first, second, or third level according to the three-story intellect verbs (p. 38). Tally the results.

   a. Number of first-story gathering questions. _____

   b. Number of second-story processing questions. _____

   c. Number of third-story applying questions. _____

2. Analyze a chapter test from a book or any commercially made content test along the same guidelines as question one. Tally the results.

   a. Number of first-story gathering questions. _____

   b. Number of second-story processing questions. _____

   c. Number of third-story applying questions. _____

3. Compare and contrast the analysis of your original teacher-made test to your analysis of the commercially made test. Comment on your findings.

4. Construct an original teacher-made test to use with your students. Follow the guidelines discussed in this chapter.

IRISkyLight

RECORD

TEACHER-MADE TESTS
REFLECTION PAGE

Analyze your original teacher-made test by using "The Big Ten Teacher-Made Test Checklist" on page 40. Complete a self-evaluation of your test.

_____
_____
_____
_____
_____
_____
_____
_____
_____
_____
_____
_____
_____
_____
_____
_____
_____
_____
_____
_____
_____

IRI SkyLight

PORTFOLIOS

CHAPTER 4

"A portfolio is more than just a
container full of stuff. It's a systematic
and organized collection of evidence
used by the teacher and student to
monitor growth of the student's
knowledge, skills, and attitudes in a
specific subject area."

-Vavrus, 1990, *Instructor*, p. 48

WHAT IS A PORTFOLIO?

PAUSE

"A portfolio is more than a 'folder' of student work; it is a deliberate, specific collection of accomplishments."
-Hamm & Adams, 1991, p. 20

A portfolio is a collection of a student's work that connects separate items to form a clearer, more complete picture of the student as a lifelong learner. Portfolios can contain a repertoire of assessments such as observation checklists, logs, journals, videos, cassettes, pictures, projects, and performances. These different types of assessments allow students to display every aspect of their capabilities. A portfolio contains several separate pieces that may not mean much by themselves, but when compiled together, they produce a more accurate and holistic portrait of the student. "A portfolio is more than a 'folder' of student work; it is a deliberate, specific collection of accomplishments" (Hamm & Adams, 1991, p. 20).

Portfolios come in the form of file folders, hanging folders, notebooks, boxes, or video disks. They can include the work of one student or a group of students. They can cover one subject area or all the subject areas. They can be sent home at the end of the year or they can be stored in the school and passed on from year to year. They can include anecdotal records, whole class profiles, parent surveys, formal test results, narrative report cards, or any number of items selected by both the teacher and the student.

Elementary teachers can include all the subject areas in one portfolio. Middle school teachers could have students keep an integrated portfolio of the different subjects they take in their teams, and high school teachers can have students keep quarterly, semester, or yearly portfolios that may eventually become employment portfolios when the students graduate.

Some school systems are planning to use portfolios to monitor student growth from kindergarten to senior year. Often students leaving one grade share their portfolios with students coming into the grade so the new students know what to expect. Other systems allow students to keep their portfolios to monitor their own development over the years and to help them evaluate their own progress. Some portfolios are graded on the basis of predetermined criteria; others are used to help students reflect on their own progress and set goals for the future.

WHY SHOULD WE USE PORTFOLIOS?

Wolf (1989), Vavrus (1990), Paulson et al. (1991), Lazear (1991), and many others recommend using portfolios because they can be used as:

- Tools for discussion with peers, teachers, and parents
- Opportunities for students to demonstrate their skills and understanding
- Opportunities for students to reflect on their work
- Chances to set future goals
- Documentation of students' development and growth in ability, attitudes, and expression
- Demonstrations of different learning styles, multiple intelligences, cultural diversity
- Chances for students to make critical choices about what they select for their portfolio
- Opportunities for students to trace the development of their learning
- Opportunities for students to make connections between prior knowledge and new learning

Hansen (1992) advocates using self-created literacy portfolios where students include what they are like *outside* the classroom. Students can include pictures of relatives, awards, or ribbons they have won in athletic events, or lists of books or magazines about rock stars, sports, hobbies, or anything that interests them. The key to the portfolio is the discussion the items generate. Every adult and student in a literacy portfolios project creates a literacy portfolio. "Whether or not we know ourselves better than anyone else does, our portfolios give us the opportunity to get to know ourselves better" (Hansen, 1992, p. 66).

Krogness (1991) suggests that students list their goals at the beginning of each year. The goal setting allows them to learn what they value and address their concerns and interests by doing authentic work.

PAUSE

"Whether or not we know ourselves better than anyone else does, our portfolios give us the opportunity to get to know ourselves better."
-Hansen, 1992, p. 66

1) Best Work Portfolio
2) Integrated Portfolio (several subjects tog
3) Tech-Prep Employability
4) multi-year portfolio

HOW SHOULD WE USE PORTFOLIOS?

Portfolios can reveal a great deal about each student. They allow teachers and students to understand the educational process at the level of the individual learner. "Portfolios allow students to assume ownership in ways that few other instructional approaches allow. Portfolio assessment requires students to collect and reflect on examples of their work…. If carefully assembled, portfolios become an intersection of instruction and assessment: they are not just instruction or just assessment but, rather, both. Together, instruction and assessment give more than either gives separately" (Paulson, Paulson, and Meyer, 1991, p. 61).

Teachers need to determine many things before beginning a portfolio program. Portfolio planning needs to be done before the first portfolio assignment is given. Teachers need to know the answers to the following questions before they begin a portfolio.

Questions to Ask
Before Beginning a Portfolio System

1. What are the purposes of using a portfolio?
2. How should the pieces in the portfolio be selected?
3. What specific pieces should be included?
4. What are the evaluation options?
5. How should the portfolio be organized?
6. What are the options for conducting portfolio conferences?

The following checklists help individual teachers or groups of teachers decide how they can use portfolios to meet the needs of their students.

A. How will the portfolio be used?
1. Is the entire portfolio going to move with the student from grade to grade, school to school?
2. Will a few pieces be saved from each year as the portfolio is passed from grade to grade?
3. Will it be sent home to the parents at the end of each year?

4. Is it going to contain work from only one class (English, history), or from all the subject areas?
5. Is it going to be used as a schoolwide or districtwide accountability piece to compare students with other students using pre-established criteria?
6. Is it going to be used as a reflective piece so that students can look back at their work and see their own growth and development?
7. Will it be used for self-evaluation by the student?
8. Is it going to be used for parent conferences?
9. Have the pieces in the portfolio been graded prior to handing in the finished portfolio? (Therefore, there is no grade on the portfolio.)
10. Is it going to be assessed as part of the final grade?

B. How should the pieces in the portfolio be selected?
1. Should some works that are "still in progress" be included?
2. Should only finished products be contained in the portfolio?
3. Should students select only their "best" work?
4. Should the students select all the pieces to be included in the portfolio?
5. Should the teacher select all the pieces to be included in the portfolio?
6. Should the teachers and the students share in the selection process of the portfolio's content?
7. Should teacher comments about the students' work be included?
8. Should peer comments about the portfolio be included?

C. What specific pieces should be included in the portfolio?
1. Homework
2. Teacher-made quizzes and tests
3. Peer editing assignments
4. Group work (artifacts or pictures)
5. Learning logs
6. Problem-solving logs
7. Reflective journals
8. Community projects
9. Written work
10. Rough drafts of written work to show process
11. Cassettes of speeches, readings, singing, questioning techniques
12. Graphic organizers

1) Collect everything
2) Go back & select key items (7 to 10 items)
3) Combination of teacher & student selection
4) Selections should be made 3 to 4 times a year
5) Perfect some of the items you select
6) show drafts as well as final for some pieces
7) Students need to reflect on what they have done. (See reflect evaluation) including assessment all or some of complete portfolio
8) Set goals (projects) short & long

13. Questions for a conference
14. Questionnaires about attitudes and opinions
15. Interviews with other students
16. Observation checklists (self or group)
17. Metacognitive activities
18. Self-assessments
19. Letter to teacher or parents about contents of portfolio
20. Statement of future goals
21. Free pick (no criteria given)
22. Pictures of performances such as speeches, plays, debates, historical re-enactments
23. Pictures of individual projects or group projects that are too big to include
24. A registry or log where students date and discuss when and why they log in an entry and when they take out an entry
25. Computer programs
26. Lab experiments
27. Samples of artwork (or pictures)
28. Videos of performances

D. What are the evaluation options?

1. Students' work is assessed throughout the course. There-fore, the final portfolio is **not graded**; it is just a tool to allow students and parents to see growth and development over time.
2. **One grade** is given to the entire portfolio on the basis of the body of work included. The grade is based on criteria that have been predetermined by both the students and the teacher.
3. **Each piece** of work in the portfolio is **graded separately** on the basis of predetermined criteria for each assignment.
4. **No grade** is given on the final portfolio, but a few pieces from each subject area are collected in one integrated portfo-lio to represent the body of work of a student for a year. The portfolio is sent home to the parents or passed on to the next year's teacher.
5. **Several pieces** from the portfolio are **passed on to the next teacher** the next year. Each year some pieces will be re-moved and others will be added in order to compile a body of work for a graduating senior.
6. The **senior portfolio** is used in the interview process for a job or college.

E. How can the portfolio be organized?
1. **Creative cover** that reflects the personality or interests of the student
2. **Table of contents** that includes the items and page numbers of the pieces of work contained in the portfolio
3. The **contents** of the portfolio organized according to the table of contents
4. A **written comment** about each item in the portfolio telling why the item was selected and how the student feels about it
5. A **self-assessment** of the portfolio by the student
6. A list of **future goals** based on the students' needs, interests, and self-assessment of the portfolio
7. A **letter** from the teacher or parents to the student including comments, feedback, and encouragement

F. What are the options for conducting portfolio conferences?
1. **Student-Teacher:** The student can discuss the portfolio with the teacher.
2. **Student-Student:** Each student can share the contents of his or her portfolio with peers.
3. **Student-Cooperative Group Members:** Each member of the cooperative group can share his or her portfolio with group members.
4. **Cross-Age:** Students in one grade can share their portfolios with students in another grade.
5. **Student-Parent:** Students can conduct their own portfolio conference at home or at official school conferences.
6. **Student-Parent-Teacher:** The participants talk about portfolios at school and set up video stations to show performances and projects.
7. **Student-Parent Conference at Home:** Students take the portfolio home to show and explain to parents. A question guide helps parents ask thoughtful questions.
8. **Significant Other:** Student invites a friend, teacher, brother, sister, or parent to school for a portfolio conference during school hours or after school.
9. **Portfolio Exhibitions:** Students display portfolios at an exhibition and explain their work to visitors.
10. **Pen Pal:** Students mail a few items from portfolios to pen pals and solicit comments or suggestions.

EXAMPLES

LANGUAGE ARTS
PORTFOLIO
(INTEGRATED UNIT)

Table of Contents

1. Letter to parents
2. Book review of *Charlotte's Web*
3. Mind map of spiders
4. Water-color picture of spiders
5. Tape of me reading story
6. My original short story (first and final drafts)
7. Science report on "Arachnids"
8. Spider rap song
9. Pictures of group project on spiders
10. Reflections on my portfolio

GEOMETRY
PORTFOLIO

Table of Contents

1. My "Math Phobia" Journal
2. Two geometry tests
3. Glossary of geometry terms
4. Drawings of geometric shapes (labeled)
5. Three problem-solving logs
6. String geometric design
7. Video of group project on angles
8. Essay on video, "Why Math?"
9. Reflections on math-related careers
10. Self-assessment of portfolio

BIOLOGY
PORTFOLIO

Table of Contents

1. Report on 20 careers related to the field of Biology
2. One lab report
3. One problem-solving log
4. Pamphlet on diabetes (group project)
5. Video of group presentation on the circulatory system
6. Essay on germ warfare
7. Research paper on AIDS
8. Tape-recorded interview with college biology professor
9. Self-evaluation of portfolio
10. Future goals in science field

AMERICAN HISTORY
PORTFOLIO

Table of Contents

1. Annotated bibliographies of five books written about the Civil War
2. Reading list of 50 books and articles related to the Civil War
3. One abstract of a research article
4. Cassette recording of interview with local historian
5. Journal entries of trip to Gettysburg
6. Map of the Battle of Gettysburg
7. Video of oral presentation on Pickett's charge
8. Research paper on military tactics of the Battle of Gettysburg
9. Venn diagram comparing Battle of Gettysburg and Battle of Chancellorsville
10. Critique of TV miniseries *The Civil War*

©1993 by IRI/Skylight Publishing, Inc.

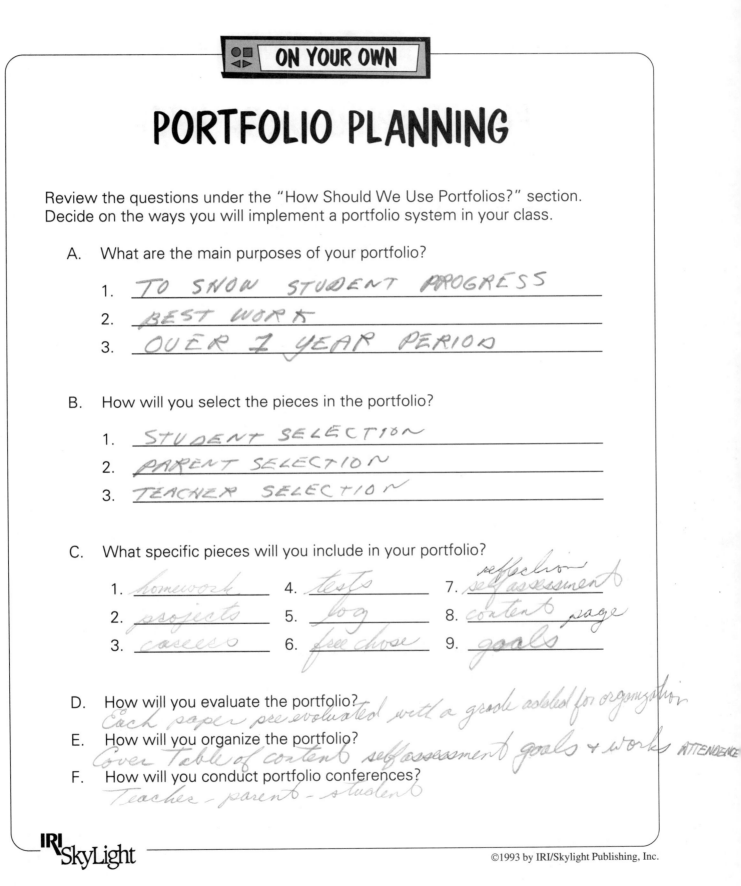

ON YOUR OWN

PORTFOLIO PLANNING

Review the questions under the "How Should We Use Portfolios?" section. Decide on the ways you will implement a portfolio system in your class.

A. What are the main purposes of your portfolio?

1. TO SHOW STUDENT PROGRESS
2. BEST WORK
3. OVER 1 YEAR PERIOD

B. How will you select the pieces in the portfolio?

1. STUDENT SELECTION
2. PARENT SELECTION
3. TEACHER SELECTION

C. What specific pieces will you include in your portfolio?

1. homework
2. projects
3. careers
4. tests
5. log
6. free chose
7. reflection self assessment
8. content page
9. goals

D. How will you evaluate the portfolio?
Each paper pre evaluated with a grade added for organization

E. How will you organize the portfolio?
Cover Table of content self assessment goals + works ATTENDENCE

F. How will you conduct portfolio conferences?
Teacher - parent - student

©1993 by IRI/Skylight Publishing, Inc.

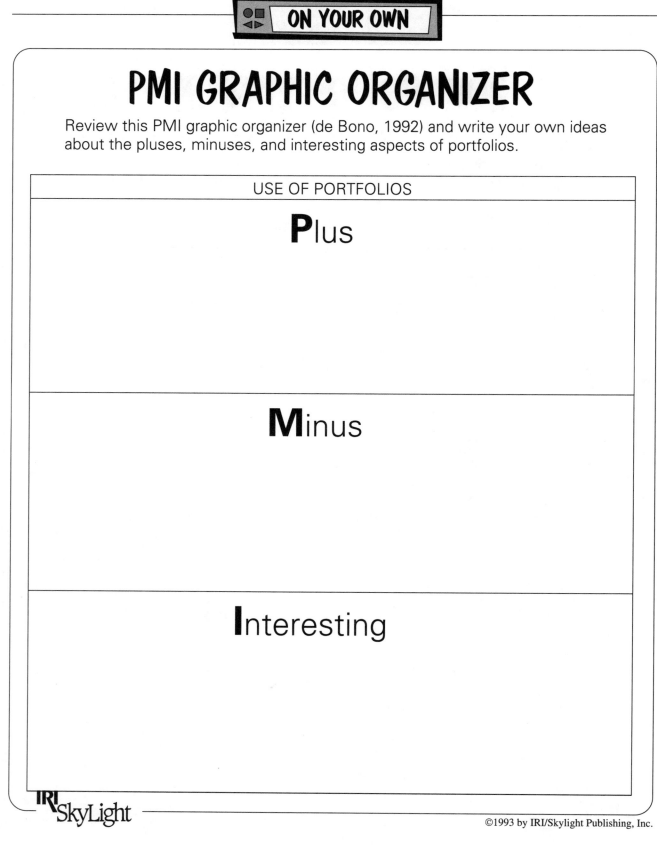

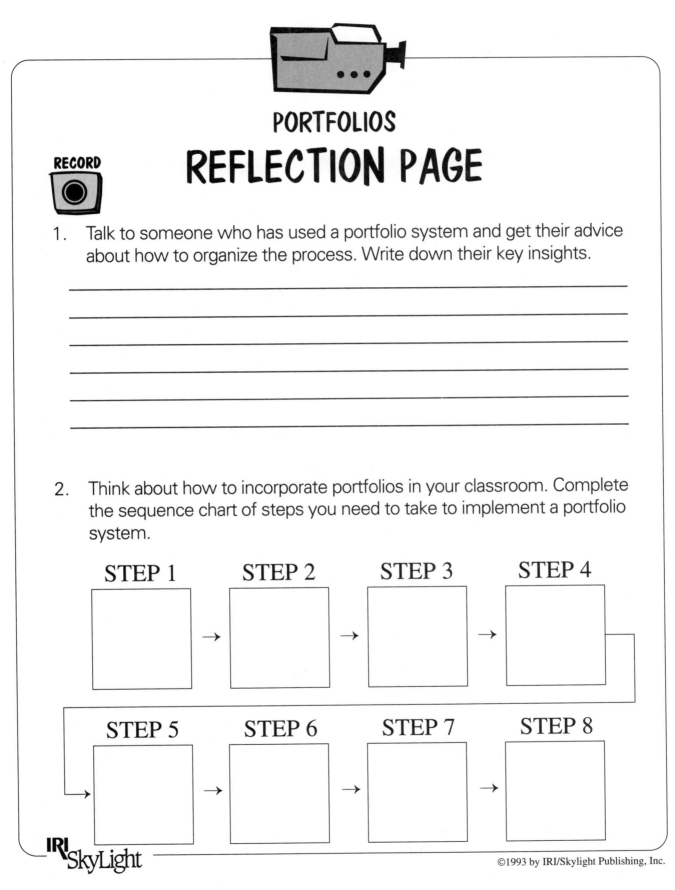

PORTFOLIOS
REFLECTION PAGE

RECORD

1. Talk to someone who has used a portfolio system and get their advice about how to organize the process. Write down their key insights.

    _____

    _____

    _____

    _____

    _____

    _____

2. Think about how to incorporate portfolios in your classroom. Complete the sequence chart of steps you need to take to implement a portfolio system.

    STEP 1 → STEP 2 → STEP 3 → STEP 4

    STEP 5 → STEP 6 → STEP 7 → STEP 8

IRI SkyLight

Notes:

_____

_____

_____

_____

_____

_____

_____

_____

_____

_____

_____

_____

_____

_____

_____

_____

_____

_____

_____

_____

_____

_____

_____

_____

_____

_____

PERFORMANCES AND EXHIBITIONS

CHAPTER 5

"The aim is to invent an authentic
simulation, and like all simulations, case
studies, or experiential exercises, the task
must be rich in contextual detail...
One must please a real audience, make a
design actually work, or achieve an
aesthetic effect that causes pride or dismay
in the result."

-Wiggins, 1992, p. 27

WHAT ARE PERFORMANCES AND EXHIBITIONS?

Performing a science experiment, defending the way students solve a problem, performing a music recital, giving a speech, and creating a newspaper are all examples of performance tasks where students exhibit what they can do. Delivering a speech about raising the driving age from sixteen to eighteen in front of an assembly program of high school students is an example of a performance that is more authentic than taking a multiple-choice test in driver's education.

PAUSE

"The criteria used to evaluate student performance are critical; in the absence of criteria, assessment remains an isolated and episodic activity."
-Marshall, in Herman, Aschbacher, and Winters, 1992, p. vi

Performances are applications of learning and are integral in the learning and transfer process. Business leaders have been critical of education because many students enter the work force with the *knowledge base* of facts they have memorized in school, but without the ability to *perform* the tasks necessary for the job. They cannot transfer their knowledge of skills to their application of skills in situations outside the classroom.

In the area of assessment, the word "performance" goes beyond the traditional definition of formal speeches, plays, or presentations. It refers to any performance or product students create that allows them to apply and demonstrate what they have learned.

One of the most motivating aspects of performance involves the use of the exhibition. The Coalition of Essential Schools Program offers a step-by-step method that teachers can use to develop effective performance assessments that allow students to demonstrate their mastery of desired outcomes through active, multi-tasked activities. "The 'performance' aspect is what the students actually do: researching, writing, speaking publicly, participating in discussions, role playing in simulations, etc. The 'assessment' part evolves from activities and criteria which can be designed not only by the teacher but also by the teacher *and* the students" (Johnson, 1992, p. 38).

One of the key steps in designing an exhibition is the concept of "planning backwards" (McDonald as cited in Johnson, 1992). Assessment planning, therefore, begins with a "vision" of what the student's work or performance will look like in its final form. After the vision is established, it is necessary to imagine what the vision looks like. "A clearly defined final exhibition, delineating *exactly* what is required of students must be presented *before* any work is assigned or begun. This would carefully explain to students the content to be covered, the skills that must be learned, applied, and mastered, and the behaviors (individually and in the context of the class or school community) students would be expected to exhibit publicly by a specific deadline" (Johnson, 1992, p. 39).

Sizer and Rogers (1993) describe a seventh grade exhibition where two teams of students conduct the 1944 Korematsu Case before the Supreme Court. One side challenges the Roosevelt Executive Order requiring internment of Japanese Americans during World War II. The jury is made up of the teacher, the principal, and parents. "This trial is a public exhibition of mastery. Because it draws on various modes of expression, the performance offers a glimpse of a rich cross section of a child's skills and abilities. Through the interchange among participants, we can see each child's progress, and make a fairer, more useful assessment of the students' abilities than traditional assessment would allow" (Sizer & Rogers, 1993, p. 26).

Mock trials, science fairs, and debates are all examples of performances and exhibitions that genuinely reflect whether students really know what they have been taught.

Asking students to perform is certainly not an innovative educational strategy; teachers have been assigning performances for years. What has been missing in many cases, however, is the development of the criteria by which the performances are assessed. "The criteria used to evaluate student performance are critical; in the absence of criteria, assessment remains an isolated and episodic activity" (Marshall, in Herman, Aschbacher, and Winters, 1992, p. vi).

PAUSE

"Because it draws on various modes of expression, the performance offers a glimpse of a rich cross section of a child's skills and abilities."
-Sizer & Rogers, 1993, p. 26

WHY SHOULD WE USE PERFORMANCES AND EXHIBITIONS?

"There is, I think, no point in the philosophy of progressive education which is sounder than its emphasis upon the importance of the participation of the learner in the formation of the purposes which direct his activities in the learning process..." (Dewey, 1938, p. 67).

Current research confirms Dewey's philosophy of active learning. Performances and exhibitions motivate students to get involved and to take ownership in the learning process. If these performances are structured effectively, they will include many or all of the thoughtful learner outcomes students need to attain. In the process of preparing an exhibition like the Korematsu Case before the Supreme Court described by Sizer and Rogers (1993), students may achieve some of the following outcomes:

Learner Outcomes from Exhibitions
1. Accessing information
2. Use of technology
3. Collaboration
4. Higher-order thinking skills
5. Problem solving
6. Written and oral communication
7. Reflection on ethical issues
8. Persistence
9. Appreciation of disparate value systems
10. Decision making
11. Conflict resolution

Even though performances and exhibitions take longer to prepare and present than traditional lecture and paper-and-pencil activities, they focus on helping students achieve the thoughtful outcomes that transfer to life.

"The philosophical cornerstone of performance assessment is 'knowledge in use'" (Johnson, 1992, p. 43). Students can construct learning in the context of the real world in order to understand what they are learning. Performances and exhibitions represent a culminating experience where students show mastery of what they have learned.

PAUSE

"The philosophical cornerstone of performance assessment is 'knowledge in use'."
-Johnson, 1992, p. 43

HOW SHOULD WE ASSESS PERFORMANCES AND EXHIBITIONS?

Many teachers avoid assigning performances because they do not feel comfortable grading them. Objective-style tests are easy to grade; they are short, and, of course, they are *objective*. Performances, on the other hand, are more difficult to grade; they are longer and more *subjective*. How many times has a teacher heard a student's oral presentation only to agonize over what grade to give? It is difficult to know how hard the student worked preparing the speech and how difficult it was for him or her to speak in front of the class. Should effort count? How do I grade fairly? Do I adjust for ability levels? Do I base it on specific criteria or just "gut reaction" and instinct? Because of the problems inherent in assigning grades and the time constraints of hearing thirty-five oral presentations, teachers often require few presentations or require presentations devoid of predetermined standards and criteria. It is no wonder that the students, parents, and sometimes even the teachers feel unsure about the grading methods used.

The key to effective performances is setting the standards and criteria in advance. "In the absence of criteria, assessment tasks remain just that, tasks or instructional activities. Perhaps most important, scoring criteria make public what is being judged and, in many cases, the standards for acceptable performance. Thus, criteria communicate your goals and achievement standards" (Herman, Aschbacher, and Winters, 1992, p. 44). A rubric refers to the scoring form that contains the criteria to be judged. Examples of scoring rubrics appear on page 67.

According to Simmons and Resnick, "performance standards provide examples and explicit definitions of what students must do to show that they have learned to an adequate level of specified skills, strategies, and knowledge" (1993, p. 12). These standards provide a benchmark whereby students see examples to which they can compare themselves.

Benchmarks or *standards* are models that teachers, parents, and students can refer to when designing, implementing, and assessing student outcomes. The city of Toronto developed more than 100 benchmarks because teachers "had few moorings to secure their

PAUSE

"...scoring criteria make public what is being judged and, in many cases, the standards for acceptable performance."
-Herman, Aschbacher, and Winters, 1992, p. 44

judgments about student achievement. For parents, there were no guarantees that teachers would not evaluate students either too rigorously or too leniently" (Larter and Donnelly, 1993, p. 59).

Clear criteria communicate to students what is expected of them. They are woven into the assignment and the assessment so that students are aware of their goals and expectations. The students, therefore, become a part of the process of determining what constitutes a good performance. "Your criteria need to make sense to students so that they will be able to apply them easily to their own work and become self-regulated learners" (Herman, Aschbacher, and Winters, 1992, p. 77).

CONTROVERSY OVER UNIFORM STANDARDS

Kallick agrees that students need to be a part of the establishment of criteria for performances. She says that one of the most significant forces that motivate a student to learn in school is the student's discovery of his or her capacity to do successful and good work. She suggests that how one determines whether a student is doing successful work should be a collaborative process of standard setting. "In most educational settings this is not the case. Rather, standards for successful and good work are set outside of the student's own sense of performance. The standards are presented to the student as an immutable fact, non-negotiable regardless of the student's justifiable reasoning about his or her own performance. When students are brought into a dialogue about standards, ownership of the evaluative data is more successful" (Kallick, 1992, p. 314).

Eisner (1993) also questions the idea of applying uniform standards to all students because he thinks assessment ought to take into account other considerations. He feels that by creating one standard for every student, students will suffer from the same problems they do now from standardized tests. "Experienced and skilled teachers know that when they appraise a student's work, they need to consider where that student started, the amount of practice and effort expended, the student's age and developmental level, and the extent to which his or her current work displays progress. Although such considerations are not particularly relevant for praising the work of professionals, they are relevant for appraising the educational development of the student" (Eisner, 1993, p. 23).

PAUSE

"When students are brought into a dialogue about standards, ownership of the evaluative data is more successful." -Kallick, 1992, p. 314

Eisner is also concerned about standardization in the schools. He says the preoccupation with uniform standards, common national goals, curriculum, and achievement tests may not improve education. "We need to celebrate diversity and to cultivate the idiosyncratic aptitudes our students possess" (Eisner, 1993, p. 23).

Some educators suggest assigning two grades to each student. One grade would measure how the student has developed and what progress he or she has made, and the other grade would show how he or she measures up to the standards for his or her age group. Regardless of the controversy about whether standards should be developed outside or inside the classroom, teachers and students can learn from the national standards, benchmarks, and exemplars of excellence and use them as models or goals.

PAUSE

"We need to celebrate diversity and to cultivate the idiosyncratic aptitudes our students possess."
-Eisner, 1993, p. 23

The First Portfolio

Reprinted with permission from Art Bouthillier.

"I kept saying, 'Maybe we should clean off the front of the refrigerator'—but, nooo. . ."

GUIDELINES FOR
PERFORMANCES AND EXHIBITIONS

1. Make sure the performance is correlated with meaningful learner outcomes.

2. Introduce the performance by telling students why they will be doing the task and what the intended outcome is (e.g., the development of communication or problem-solving skills).

3. Model or show examples or video performances from other classes or real-life presentations. (Try to show examples that are "Not Yet," those that are "O.K.," as well as those that are "Awesome.")

4. Brainstorm a list of criteria that make up a performance (e.g., eye contact, gestures, voice, enthusiasm, visual aids, organization, research).

5. Generate a list of indicators that specify the types of performances under each of the examples.

6. Create a scale that lists the indicators for each of the criteria on the scale (Not Yet, O.K., Awesome).

7. Give students some choice in their selection of topics.

8. Encourage students to plan, monitor, and evaluate their thinking in the process (metacognition).

9. Have students give the performance.

10. Have students share the performance with the class and or outside audience (other classes, parents, school).

11. Ask peers to evaluate the performance.

12. Have the student self-evaluate by viewing the videotape of the performance.

13. Use the criteria to complete a teacher evaluation.

14. Discuss performance with student.

15. Provide feedback.

16. Determine a grade based on the peer, self-, and teacher evaluations.

17. Have the student set new goals for his or her next performance.

18. Save the critiques of the speech, the videotape, and the student's list of future goals to include in the portfolio.

Types of Scoring Devices

Numerical scales assign points to a continuum of performance levels. According to Herman, Aschbacher, and Winters (1992), the length of the continuum or the number of scale points can vary from three to seven or more. However, a shorter scale will result in a high percent agreement and a larger scale will take longer to reach consensus if more than one person is evaluating the performance.

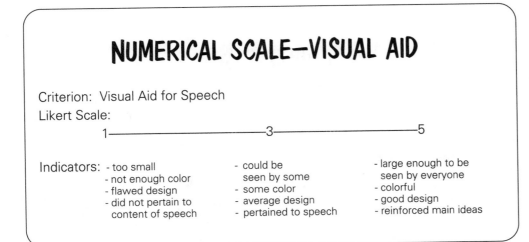

NUMERICAL SCALE—VISUAL AID

Criterion: Visual Aid for Speech

Likert Scale:

1————————————3————————————5

Indicators:
- too small
  - not enough color
  - flawed design
  - did not pertain to content of speech

- could be seen by some
- some color
- average design
- pertained to speech

- large enough to be seen by everyone
- colorful
- good design
- reinforced main ideas

PAUSE

Numerical scales assign points to a continuum of performance levels.

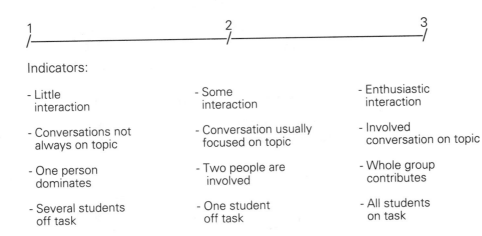

NUMERICAL SCALE—COLLABORATION

Criterion: Collaboration in Cooperative Groups

1————————————2————————————3

Indicators:

- Little interaction

- Conversations not always on topic

- One person dominates

- Several students off task

- Some interaction

- Conversation usually focused on topic

- Two people are involved

- One student off task

- Enthusiastic interaction

- Involved conversation on topic

- Whole group contributes

- All students on task

Qualitative scales use adjectives rather than numbers to characterize student performance. There are two types of qualitative scales: descriptive and evaluative.

Descriptive scales label student performance by using fairly neutral terms to characterize the performance. They do not always make explicit the standards on which the judgment is based.

PAUSE

Descriptive scales label student performance by using fairly neutral terms to characterize the performance.

DESCRIPTIVE SCALE

"No evidence… Minimal evidence… Partial evidence… Complete evidence.

Task not attempted… Partial completion… Completed… Goes beyond.

Off task… Attempts to address task… Minimal attention to task… Addresses task but no elaboration… Fully elaborated and attentive to task and audience."

(Herman, Aschbacher, and Winters, 1992, p. 67)

The state of Kentucky is using a descriptive scale on their performance levels of student assessment. They have also included graphics showing a range from a seedling to a full-grown tree to illustrate growth. "In the new assessment program, no child 'fails.' Instead the assessment results place him or her into one of four performance levels: novice, apprentice, proficient, or distinguished. The lowest level, novice, recognizes the child as a beginner, not a failure" (1991, Kentucky Department of Education).

Evaluative scales incorporate judgments of worth based on standards of excellence. The most commonly used evaluative scores are grades. Other evaluative scales use descriptors of excellence or judgment of competence. These scales require scoring criteria that include standards of excellence, competence, or significant outcomes (Herman, Aschbacher, and Winters, 1992).

EVALUATIVE SCALE

A	Student addressed topic logically and used effective delivery style to present case.
B	Student addressed topic in organized way and used effective speaking techniques.
C	Student addressed topic but did not use effective speaking techniques (eye contact, gestures).
D	Student did not address the topic.
F	Student did not give speech.

PAUSE

"In the new assessment program, no child 'fails.'. . . The lowest level, novice, recognizes the child as a beginner, not a failure."
-Boysen, 1992

Mrs. Grizlow was not amused when her students practiced their scoring rubric on her spring wardrobe.

LIKERT SCALES
THAT CAN BE USED FOR ASSESSMENT

Students and teachers can develop their own Likert scales that reflect their personalities and interests. The following examples may be more descriptive to students than numbers and they also show growth on a continuum scale.

1) Criterion: _____

/————————————————/————————————————/
  Not Yet   Not Bad   Ah hah!
-                        •   •
-                        •   •
-                        •   •

2) Criterion: _____

/————————————————/————————————————/
  Out of the Gate   2nd Lap   Home Stretch
-                        •   •
-                        •   •
-                        •   •

3) Criterion: _____

/————————————————/————————————————/
  It's Greek   The Fog is   Yes-Yes-Yes!
  to Me   Lifting
-                        •   •
-                        •   •
-                        •   •

4) Criterion: _____

/————————————————/————————————————/
  On the Bench   Rounding 2nd   Home Run!
-                        •   •
-                        •   •
-                        •   •

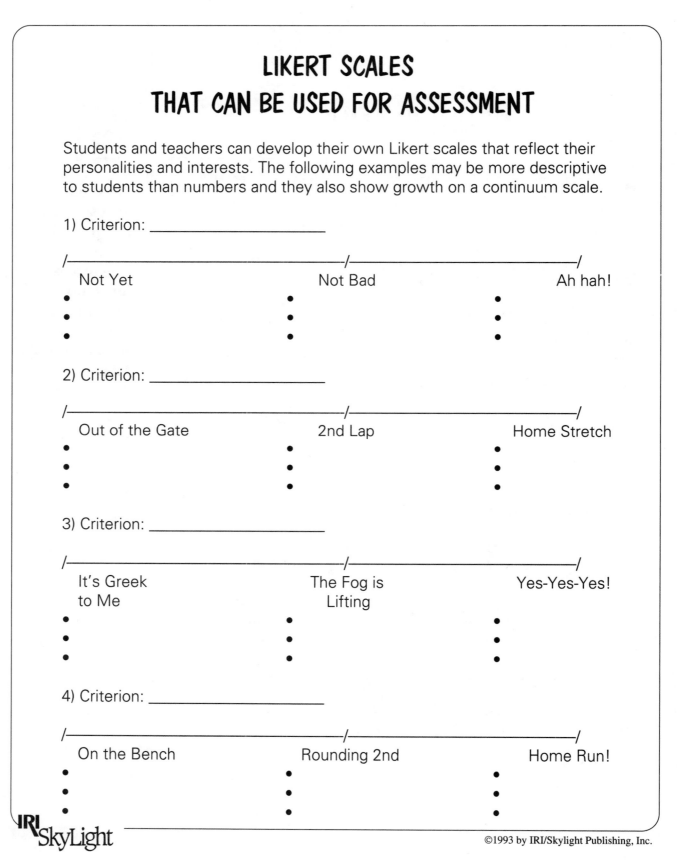

IRI/SkyLight

EXAMPLES

VERBAL SKILLS RUBRIC

Name: Mary   Date: May 19

1. **ORAL LANGUAGE**
   1———————③———————5
   Non-Verbal   Talks with   Speaks in
   in Class   Friends   Sentences
                                        in Class

2. **READING**
   1———————③———————5
   Reads Own   Knows Key   Sounds Out
   Name   Words   Words

3. **WRITING**
   ①———————3———————5
   Scribbles   Can Write   Can Write
                     First Name   Words

GROUP PROJECT RUBRIC

Name: Sue, Pete, and Joe   Date: November 5
Topic: Historical Re-Enactment of the Scopes Monkey Trial

Check one type of assessment:
❏ Self   ☒ Group   ❏ Teacher

1. **Criterion: Accuracy of Information**
   1————2————3————④————5
   Smattering of   Round of   Standing
   Applause   Applause   Ovation

2. **Criterion: Costumes**
   1————2————3————④————5
   Smattering of   Round of   Standing
   Applause   Applause   Ovation

3. **Criterion: Dialogue**
   1————2————3————4————⑤
   Smattering of   Round of   Standing
   Applause   Applause   Ovation

4. **Criterion: Acting Ability**
   1————2————3————④————5
   Smattering of   Round of   Standing
   Applause   Applause   Ovation

Total Grade= 17 points divided by 4 = 4.2

SCALE	
4.5 – 5 =	A
3.8 – 4.4 =	B
2.8 – 3.7 =	C
2 – 2.7 =	D
Below 2 =	Not yet

Comments: Your group created costumes and dialogue that enhanced your performance. You had two factual errors in your courtroom scene that lowered your accuracy grade. Also, two characters had trouble remembering their lines.

ORAL PRESENTATION RUBRIC

Name: Mary   Date: October 3
Subject: Science Project   Final Grade: 4

5	The subject is addressed clearly Speech is loud enough and easy to understand Good eye contact Visual aid is used effectively Well-organized
④	Subject is addressed adequately Speech has appropriate volume Eye contact is intermittent Visual aid helps presentations Good organization
3	Subject is addressed adequately Speech volume is erratic Student reads notes—erratic eye contact Visual aid does not enhance speech Speech gets "off track" in places
2	Speech needs more explanation Speech is difficult to understand at times Lack of adequate eye contact Poor visual aid Lack of organization
1	Speech does not address topic Speech cannot be heard Very little eye contact No visual aid No organization

Scale: 5 = A; 4 = B; 3 = C; 2 = D; 1 = Not Yet
General Comments: You did a good job demonstrating your project and delivering the speech. Your organization, however, was a little sloppy and you read your notes too much.

WEIGHTED WRITING RUBRIC

Name: Mary   Date: May 23
Piece of Writing: Persuasive Paper

Score   Score: 1   2   3   4   5
(1-5)   Low   High

CONTENT • evidence of reason ◉ key ideas covered • appropriate quotes - Not enough • supportive statistics • topic addressed	Score 4	x 7 = 28 (35)
ORGANIZATION • creative introduction • thesis statement • appropriate support statements • effective transition	Score 5	x 6 = 30 (30)
USAGE ◉ correct subject-verb agreement - 2 errors • no run-ons, fragments, or comma splices • correct verb tense • mix of simple and complex sentences	Score 3	x 5 = 15 (25)
MECHANICS • few or no misspellings • correct use of punctuation • correct use of capitalization	Score 5	x 2 = 10 (10)
Scale: 93–100=A, 87–92=B, 78–86=C	TOTAL SCORE:	83 (100)

Comments: Your content and organization are good, but you need to work on your sentence structure. 1 comma splice.

IRI SkyLight

ON YOUR OWN

EVALUATION SCALE EXAMPLE

Directions: Select a perfomance you would assign your students and decide on three criteria and the indicators under each score.

Name: _____ Date: _____

Class: _____ Assignment: _____

CHECK ONE TYPE OF ASSESSMENT: ❑ **SELF**   ❑ **GROUP**   ❑ **TEACHER**

1. CRITERION: _____

1————————————3————————————5

- _____   - _____   - _____
- _____   - _____   - _____
- _____   - _____   - _____

2. CRITERION: _____

1————————————3————————————5

- _____   - _____   - _____
- _____   - _____   - _____
- _____   - _____   - _____

3. CRITERION: _____

1————————————3————————————5

- _____   - _____   - _____
- _____   - _____   - _____
- _____   - _____   - _____

Comments: _____
_____
_____

*Score:*_____

IRI SkyLight

ON YOUR OWN

EXHIBITIONS

Create one idea for an exhibition. Establish your vision of what the exhibition might look like in its final form and then "plan backwards" to decide on the content, skills, behaviors, and timelines (Johnson, 1992).

Outcomes:

Vision of Exhibition:

Content:

Skills:

Behaviors:

IRI SkyLight

PERFORMANCES AND EXHIBITIONS
REFLECTION PAGE

RECORD

1. After working with your students to create a scoring rubric for a specific performance, comment on the process. Would you make any revisions?

_____

_____

_____

_____

_____

_____

_____

_____

_____

_____

2. Reflect on the exhibition as a valuable learning and assessment tool. Predict how exhibitions will influence education in the twenty-first century.

_____

_____

_____

_____

_____

_____

_____

_____

_____

IRI SkyLight

PROJECTS

CHAPTER 6

"One of the most common and
most effective ways to provide
multiple opportunities for students
to use their strengths is through
working on projects."

-White, Blythe, and Gardner,
1992, p. 131

WHAT ARE PROJECTS?

A project is a formal assignment given to an individual student or a group of students on a topic related to the curriculum. The project may involve both in-class and out-of-class research and development. A project may include models, maps, pictures, tables, graphs, collages, photographs, plays, films, or videotapes. The project should be a learning activity, not primarily an evaluation activity (Board of Education for the City of Etobicoke, 1987).

Projects have always been a part of the curriculum. Almost every student has probably ransacked the kitchen cupboards for flour to make a dough map of some country with green food coloring for the hills and toothpick houses. More often than not parents help in the extravaganza and together parent and child work late into the night completing the project for the fifth grade geography class. Many students, however, probably do not understand or appreciate the significance of the project other than it is fun and the projects make great displays for back-to-school nights. Elementary school is full of projects that are displayed proudly in the rooms, in the halls, and especially on parent conference nights. Unfortunately, as students move on to high school, the number of creative projects decreases while the number of written research papers and multiple-choice tests increases.

Somehow, there just is no time to work on projects anymore. Projects are so difficult to grade and to store. Teachers often feel they cannot justify taking time away from the *curriculum* to indulge in these hands-on activities. Creativity is such a subjective trait to assess. Besides, don't parents do most of the projects anyway?

Despite the misgivings many teachers have, projects at all grade levels in music, media, art, science, language arts, and social studies can enhance learning and help students explore their own multiple intelligences. Projects can involve individual students, cooperative groups, whole classes, schools, and communities. Interdisciplinary projects, school exhibitions, or schoolwide community projects are all valuable assessment tools that allow students opportunities to show not only what they know but also what they can do.

Educators who want students to "produce" something themselves rather than just "reproduce" knowledge on tests incorporate mean-

PAUSE

Interdisciplinary projects, school exhibitions, or schoolwide community projects are all valuable assessment tools that allow students opportunities to show not only what they know but also what they can do.

ingful projects into their curriculum. Projects help students develop and enhance communication, technical, interpersonal, organizational, problem-solving, and decision-making skills—significant learner outcomes.

Teachers at the Key School in Indianapolis, Indiana, make projects an important part of each elementary student's experience. They have built their curriculum around the theory of multiple intelligences. (Gardner, 1991). Students take courses in standard subjects such as arithmetic, reading, and writing, but they also take courses in physical education, art, music, computers, and a foreign language. They draw on their own multiple intelligences and their course work to create three major projects each year.

They are encouraged to be creative and personal in developing their projects, and they also work cooperatively with other students for extended periods of time. All students present their work to fellow classmates and document their process and product on videotape so they can analyze and reflect on their own performance. The students at Key School do acquire the basic skills and the significant outcomes required of public school, but they are also able to take advantage of their personal and creative talents in the process (White, Blythe, and Gardner, 1992).

WHY SHOULD WE USE PROJECTS?

Learner outcomes are important for all students to achieve, but educators must respect the diversity of students and understand that not all students can achieve the same outcomes in the same way. Gardner's theory of multiple intelligences maintains that people possess several different capacities for creating products and solving problems. The data from his research yield evidence for at least seven discrete domains of human achievement:

- *Linguistic intelligence* involves ease in producing language (writers, poets, storytellers).
- *Logical-mathematical intelligence* involves the ability to reason and to recognize abstract patterns (scientists, mathematicians).
- *Musical intelligence* includes sensitivity to pitch and rhythm (composers, instrumentalists).

PAUSE

Projects help students develop and enhance communication, technical, interpersonal, organizational, problem-solving, and decision-making skills—significant learner outcomes.

- *Spatial intelligence* is the ability to create visual-spatial representations of the world and to transfer those representations either mentally or concretely (architects, sculptors, engineers).
- *Bodily/Kinesthetic intelligence* involves using the body to solve problems, to create products, and to convey ideas and emotions (athletes, surgeons, dancers).
- *Interpersonal intelligence* is the ability to understand other people and to work effectively with them (salespeople, teachers, politicians).
- *Intrapersonal intelligence* is personal knowledge about one's own emotions or self.

(White, Blythe, and Gardner, 1992, p. 128)

Most teachers tend to use verbal/linguistic or logical/mathematical intelligences when they teach because either that is how they were taught or that is how they learn best. Because each student has different strengths for experiencing learning, a presentation of the curriculum using only language and logic would not be equally successful for all students. Each student will construct knowledge for him- or herself depending on how he or she experiences the new material (White, Blythe, and Gardner, 1992).

PAUSE

Most teachers tend to use verbal/linguistic or logical/ mathematical intelligences when they teach because either that is how they were taught or that is how they learn best.

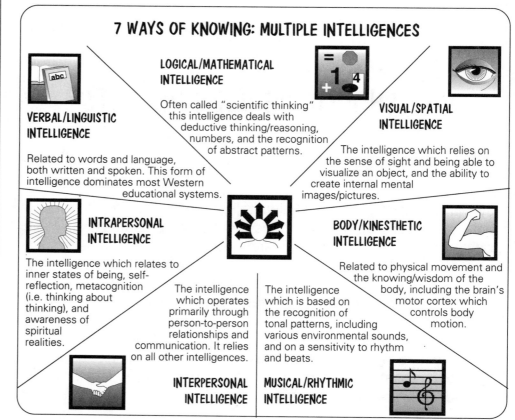

7 WAYS OF KNOWING: MULTIPLE INTELLIGENCES

LOGICAL/MATHEMATICAL INTELLIGENCE
Often called "scientific thinking" this intelligence deals with deductive thinking/reasoning, numbers, and the recognition of abstract patterns.

VERBAL/LINGUISTIC INTELLIGENCE
Related to words and language, both written and spoken. This form of intelligence dominates most Western educational systems.

VISUAL/SPATIAL INTELLIGENCE
The intelligence which relies on the sense of sight and being able to visualize an object, and the ability to create internal mental images/pictures.

INTRAPERSONAL INTELLIGENCE
The intelligence which relates to inner states of being, self-reflection, metacognition (i.e. thinking about thinking), and awareness of spiritual realities.

BODY/KINESTHETIC INTELLIGENCE
Related to physical movement and the knowing/wisdom of the body, including the brain's motor cortex which controls body motion.

The intelligence which operates primarily through person-to-person relationships and communication. It relies on all other intelligences.

The intelligence which is based on the recognition of tonal patterns, including various environmental sounds, and on a sensitivity to rhythm and beats.

INTERPERSONAL INTELLIGENCE

MUSICAL/RHYTHMIC INTELLIGENCE

(excerpted from Lazear, 1991)

74

ADVANTAGES OF THE PROJECT ASSIGNMENT

A great deal of time and effort goes into producing a quality project. Teachers should allow some class time to work on the project and the criteria for grading should be determined prior to starting the project by the teacher and students working together.

The project assignment:
1. allows students to formulate their own questions and then try to find answers to them;
2. provides students with opportunities to use their multiple intelligences to create a product;
3. allows teachers to assign projects at different levels of difficulty to account for individual learning styles and ability levels;
4. can be motivating to students;
5. provides an opportunity for positive interaction and collaboration among peers;
6. provides an alternative for students who have problems reading and writing;
7. increases the self-esteem of students who would not get recognition on tests or traditional writing assignments;
8. allows for students to share their learning and accomplishments with other students, classes, parents, or community members; and
9. can achieve essential learning outcomes through application and transfer.

HOW SHOULD WE USE PROJECTS?

The most effective way to introduce projects is to provide samples or models of completed projects. Instead of showing students only the superior models, let them see samples of some "O.K." projects and some "Not Yet" ones. After they examine the various projects, ask them to list the characteristics of each.

Once students have decided what type of project they want to complete, let them come up with criteria that play an important part

PAUSE

The project assignment increases the self-esteem of students who would not get recognition on tests or traditional writing assignments.

in the project. For example, if students want to make a video, they can view several videos and then determine the components. They might decide sound, color, narration, organization, and camera work are all essential criteria. They can then develop a rating scale or rubric to list the major criteria and the specific indicators that support the rating score. The characteristics of the superior video they viewed should serve as the benchmarks by which to measure a superior or 5 rating. After they list those indicators, they can rate their projects on a continuum or Likert scale to show growth and development.

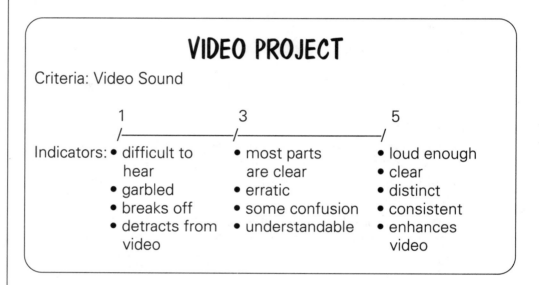

VIDEO PROJECT

Criteria: Video Sound

1	3	5
Indicators: • difficult to hear • garbled • breaks off • detracts from video	• most parts are clear • erratic • some confusion • understandable	• loud enough • clear • distinct • consistent • enhances video

PAUSE

The indicators created by students may not be as sophisticated and measurable as standardized rubrics at first, but students will soon develop a more precise vocabulary and a more accurate scoring rubric.

In addition to the student-generated scale, teachers can also use a standardized rubric from a state or district to assess a project according to established standards. The standardized rubric, however, may not be as meaningful because (a) someone from "up above" created the criteria; (b) it may not fit the ability level of the group; (c) students had no input in the process; (d) the vocabulary and wording may not make sense to the students.

The indicators created by students may not be as sophisticated and measurable as standardized rubrics at first, but students will soon develop a more precise vocabulary and a more accurate scoring rubric. They will improve their model as they are exposed to other benchmark models. Again, if students are to construct knowledge for themselves, they need to be a part of the assessment process. They need to understand the components of a good project and then use the indicators to guide them in their preparation. Wiggins says that this process will demystify tasks and standards for learners.

INDIVIDUAL AND GROUP PROJECT IDEAS

WRITTEN WORK:
Newspaper from a time period
Diary of a famous person
Writing portfolio
In-class group essay
Take-home group essay
Poetry notebook
- Haiku
- limerick
- free verse
- formula poem

Analyses of fiction profile
- short story
- novel
- drama

Original prose
Expository writing notebook
- description
- narrative
- comparison/contrast

Soap opera parody
Research report
Critical paper
Autobiography
Biography of famous person
Book review
Peer editing critiques
Letter to parents, editor, TV station
Job description of the perfect job
Diary from a historical period
Original fairy tale
Parody of a famous fairy tale
Parody of author's style (Poe, Hemingway, Faulkner)
Parody of classic literature (*The Scarlet Letter, Moby Dick*)
Original myth from a country
A modern-day myth
A legal brief of a case
Math problem-solving logs
Case study
Annotated list of books read
Graphs, charts, diagrams
Results of surveys
Pen-pal letters

Resume
Movie review
Compact disk review
Album review
Review of a TV program
Original recipes
How-to book
Pamphlet describing a disease
Vacation brochure

MEDIA:
Videotape of students' performance
Critique of videotaped performance
Cassette tape of readings or oral performances
Computer printout or disk
Video of news program
Video of original commercial
Cassettes, filmstrips, slides, transparencies, pictures or videos on cooperative group work, oral presentations, debates, student-conducted interviews, historical re-enactments

KINESTHETIC:
Pantomime
Dance routine
Exercise routine
Aerobic routine
Write and perform a song as a mnemonic device
TV commercial

ARTWORK:
Portfolio
Drawing
Collage
Critique of artwork
Illustration of a story in sequence
Comic strip
Mural
Graphic organizers
Clay models

ORAL WORK:
Conference with parents, teacher, other students
Student-conducted interview
Oral exam
Role-playing
Skit
Panel discussion
TV talk show
Man-on-the-street interview
Oral history of an event
Debate
Extemporaneous speaking
Peer tutoring
Telephone interview
News report

OTHER PROJECTS:
Artifacts
Scrapbook
Model building
Costume of characters or countries
Crossword puzzle
Mobile
Flannel board story
Food of a country or time period
Map of a country
Model of building, castle, bridge, etc.
Simulation game
"Me Bag" for introduction
Advertising campaign for a product
Puppet show

PAUSE

Classroom projects can be more authentic when students are given a chance to think about how they approach learning tasks and to communicate how they plan, monitor, and evaluate their thinking.

GUIDELINES FOR PROJECTS

Classroom projects can be more authentic with the following guidelines:

1. A variety of meaningful, long-term projects are used throughout the year.

2. Students are given some choices on the projects.

3. Students can use their multiple intelligences.

4. Learner outcomes are listed and monitored.

5. Students are provided opportunities to engage in problem solving, decision making, and other higher-order thinking skills.

6. Specific criteria for the assignment are developed by the students and the teacher. Criteria for projects may include some of the following: timeliness, appearance, originality, quality, evidence of understanding, reflection, artistic presentation, transfer of skills, organization, richness of ideas, and presentation.

7. Due dates are listed (it might be better to assign due dates for parts of the assignment rather than just the final due date for the entire assignment).

8. Students are given a chance to think about how they approach learning tasks and to communicate how they plan, monitor, and evaluate their thinking (reflection and metacognition).

9. Specific indicators under each criterion are used by students, peers, and teachers to assess the final project.

10. Teacher and student feedback is prompt, positive, and specific.

11. Students have a chance to share their work with others.

12. The student has an opportunity for self-evaluation.

EXAMPLES

MYTHOLOGICAL RAP SONG

Assignment: Students will work in groups to write and present a rap song about the gods and goddesses in Greek mythology.

SCORING RUBRIC

1. Criterion: **Accuracy of Information**

Not Yet	Almost There	Yes-Yes-Yes!
Many factual errors	Some errors	No errors

2. Criterion: **Music (Words, beat, rhythm)**

Not Yet	Almost There	Yes-Yes-Yes!
Words & music do not match	Some problems	Everything jives

3. Criterion: **Costumes**

Not Yet	Almost There	Yes-Yes-Yes!
Costumes do not match gods	Some costumes appropriate	All costumes are appropriate

4. Criterion: **Presentation**

Not Yet	Almost There	Yes-Yes-Yes!
Needs more rehearsal	Some glitches	It all gels

COMMENTS: *You did an excellent job creating the music and costumes and singing the song. You did, however, confuse Zeus and Apollo in some of your stories.*

PAMPHLET ON A DISEASE

Assignment: Each group selects and researches a disease and prepares an instructional pamphlet to present to the class.

SCORING RUBRIC

1. Criterion: **Quality of Research**

1	2	3	4	(5)
1 Source		3 Sources		5 Sources

2. Criterion: **Question and Answer Section**

1	2	3	(4)	5
Many factual errors		Some factual errors		No factual errors

3. Criterion: **Graphics**

1	2	(3)	4	5
No graphics		Graphics that explain disease		Graphics that instruct as well as dazzle!

4. Criterion: **Organization**

1	2	3	(4)	5
Little evidence		Some evidence		Strong evidence

5. Criterion: **Oral Presentation**

1	2	3	(4)	5
Did little to explain disease		Explained disease adequately		Grabbed everyone's atttention

COMMENTS: *You need to use more computer graphics to make your pamphlet more attractive. Good research and presentation.*

Grading Scale:	**Group Grade**	
	22–25	points = A
Final	18–21	points = B
Score	13–17	points = C
20 = B	8–12	points = D
	7 or below	Not Yet

VIDEOTAPE COMMUNITY PROJECT

Group: _Mary, Sam, Pete_   Date: _November 3_
Type of Project: _Videotape of Community Project_

Evaluation: ☐ Teacher   ☒ Group members   ☐ Self
Brief Description: We videotaped students in our class who spent Saturdays volunteering at a retirement home.

CRITERIA WE DEVELOPED FOR ASSESSMENT:

1. CONTENT: Did we include key scenes that conveyed the relationships between the students and the elderly people they helped?

Little Evidence	**X** — Some Evidence	Much Evidence

2. NARRATION: Did we frame the pictures with words that captured the tone and emotion of the scenes?

Little Evidence	**X** Some Evidence	Much Evidence

3. SOUND: Was the narration and the dialogue in the video clear and distinct?

Little Evidence	Some Evidence **X**	Much Evidence

4. PHOTOGRAPHY: Did the camera work to enhance the video?

Little Evidence	Some Evidence **X**	Much Evidence

5. MUSIC: Did the background music contribute to the video's overall effectiveness?

Little Evidence	Some Evidence **X**	Much Evidence

COMMENTS: We need to work on our narration because it detracts from the video.

THE MEETING OF THE MINDS

Assignment: Each student will select a famous writer, artist, politician, or philosopher from the Renaissance period and become that person on a panel of experts.

SCORING RUBRIC

1. Criterion: **Research on person and time period**

Not Yet	D	C	B	(A)
Little Evidence		Some Evidence		Much Evidence

2. Criterion: **Responses to questions addressed to panel member**

Not Yet	D	C	B	(A)
Incorrect Responses		Adequate Responses		Competent Responses

3. Criterion: **Costume and props for person from the Renaissance**

Not Yet	D	(C)	B	A
None		Questionable		Authentic

4. Criterion: **Closing Statements**

Not Yet	D	C	B	(A)
No Statement		Adequate Closing Statement		Commendable Closing Statement

COMMENTS: *It is evident that your knowledge of Dante is extensive. You responded to questions beautifully. Perhaps, however, you could have brought another prop besides a book of matches to symbolize the inferno!*

Grading Scale:		
A = 5	Total Score:	18
B = 4		
C = 3	+ 4 grades:	4.5
D = 2		
Not Yet = 1	Final Grade:	B+

IRI SkyLight

ON YOUR OWN

CREATE A PROJECT

1. Develop a list of meaningful projects that will challenge and motivate your students.

   _____

   _____

   _____

   _____

   _____

   _____

   _____

   _____

2. Select *one* of the projects you listed and answer the following questions about it:

   a. What learner outcomes will be addressed by this project?

   b. What kinds of choices will students have?

   c. What types of multiple intelligences will students be able to demonstrate by doing this project?

   d. What criteria should be assessed in this project?

IRI SkyLight

GROUP PROJECT RUBRIC

Class: _____ Type of Project:_____

Students:_____ Date:_____

Criterion #1: _____
1   2   3
/_____/_____/

INDICATORS

- •   •   •
- •   •   •
- •   •   •

Criterion #2: _____
1   2   3
/_____/_____/

INDICATORS

- •   •   •
- •   •   •
- •   •   •

Criterion #3: _____
1   2   3
/_____/_____/

INDICATORS

- •   •   •
- •   •   •
- •   •   •

Criterion #4: _____
1   2   3
/_____/_____/

INDICATORS

- •   •   •
- •   •   •
- •   •   •

Comments:_____

_____

IRI SkyLight

©1993 by IRI/Skylight Publishing, Inc.

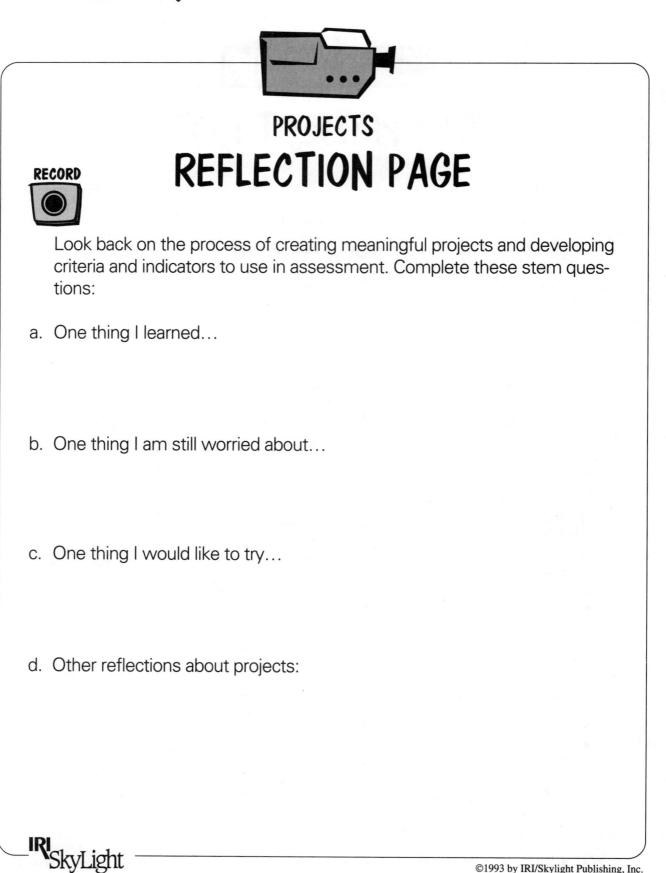

RECORD

PROJECTS
REFLECTION PAGE

Look back on the process of creating meaningful projects and developing criteria and indicators to use in assessment. Complete these stem questions:

a. One thing I learned…

b. One thing I am still worried about…

c. One thing I would like to try…

d. Other reflections about projects:

IRI SkyLight

LEARNING LOGS AND JOURNALS

CHAPTER 7

"We do not write and read primarily
in order to ensure that this nation's
employers can count on a competent,
competitive work force. We write and
read in order to know each other's
responses, to connect ourselves more
fully with the human world, and to
strengthen the habit of truth-telling in
our midst."

-DeMott, 1990, p. 6

Learning Logs used to record
- *Key ideas*
- *Questions*
- *Prediction*
- *Connections or to*
- *Summarize material*
- *keep track of progress*

WHAT ARE LEARNING LOGS AND JOURNALS?

Learning logs and reflective journals have been used by teachers as formative or ongoing assessment tools for years, but, unfortunately, mostly by teachers of English. They are, however, beginning to play an even bigger role in all of today's reflective classrooms. Logs usually consist of short, more objective entries that contain mathematics problem-solving entries, observations of science experiments, questions about the lecture or readings, lists of outside readings, homework assignments, or anything that lends itself to keeping records. The responses are usually brief, factual, and impersonal.

Journals, on the other hand, are usually written in narrative form, are more subjective, and deal more with feelings, opinions, or personal experiences. Journal entries are usually more descriptive, longer, and free-flowing than logs. They are often used to respond to pieces of literature, describe events, comment on reactions to events, reflect on personal experiences and feelings, and connect what is being studied in one class with another class or with life outside the classroom.

Research by Goodlad (1984) reveals that teachers at the high school level tend to lecture about 88% of the time. Students at all levels have attention spans from ten to twenty minutes—on good days. Therefore, not only are students "turning off" the lecture, but they are also not retaining much of what is being said. Since it is important for students to interact with the teacher, the textbook, and each other, teachers are starting to use logs and journals during lectures. They give direct instruction in chunks of ten- to fifteen-minute segments and then they ask students to write down key ideas, questions, connections, or reflections. The students can then think about the material, clarify confusion, discuss key ideas with group members, and process the information before the teacher moves on to the next segment of the direct instruction. The following is an example of such a technique.

Reflective Lesson

1. Direct instruction by teacher; lecture to the whole class. (10-15 minutes)

2. Students spend time writing in their reflective lesson log.
    (5 minutes)

REFLECTIVE LESSON LOG

Name: _____ Topic: _____ Date: _____

Key ideas from this discussion _____
_____

Connections I can make with other ideas _____
_____

Questions I still have _____
_____
_____

PAUSE

Students with special needs will have more time to process information when they use reflective logs.

3. Students then share their logs with a partner or group members. They discuss the key ideas with other students and see if they can answer each other's questions. (5 minutes)

4. The teacher conducts a brief discussion with the whole class to see if anyone still has questions that were not answered or clarified by group members. The class then discusses the connections students made with the information and "real things" in life. (5 minutes)

5. The teacher continues with the next "chunk" of direct instruction. The cycle repeats if there is time, or students complete logs for homework. Students discuss logs the following day as a review and to clarify any confusion they may have about their homework or yesterday's lesson. (10 minutes)

The advantages of structuring lessons with some built-in processing time are many:

1. Students will retain key ideas.
2. Writing skills will improve.
3. Students with special needs will have more time to process information when they use reflective logs.

4. Interaction among students will increase.
5. Students can study logs for quizzes and tests.
6. Learning logs can be included in portfolios.
7. Teachers can assign grades for selected logs or "Log Books" (daily grades or weekly grades).
8. Students who are absent can get logs from friends to keep up with work they missed.
9. Teachers can ascertain *during* the lesson if there is confusion or misunderstandings about information.
10. Teachers don't just "cover the curriculum," they select the most important information, and then they see if students understand it *before* the final test.

PAUSE

[By using logs] teachers can ascertain *during* the lesson if there is confusion or misunder-standing about information.

WHY SHOULD WE USE LEARNING LOGS AND JOURNALS?

Research by Brownlie, Close, and Wingren (1988), Jeroski, Brownlie, and Kaser (1990a), Barell (1992), Costa, Bellanca, and Fogarty (1992), and others recommends using logs and journals on a regular basis in the following ways:

1. To record *key ideas* from a lecture, movie, presentation, field trip, or reading assignments.
2. To make *predictions* about what will happen next in a story, movie, experiment, the weather, or in school, national or world events.
3. To record *questions*.
4. To *summarize* the main ideas of a book, movie, lecture, or reading.
5. To *reflect* on the information presented.
6. To *connect* the ideas presented to other subject areas or to the students' personal life.
7. To *monitor* change in an experiment or event over time.
8. To *respond* to questions posed by the teacher or other students.
9. To *brainstorm* ideas about potential projects, papers, or presentations.
10. To help *identify* problems.

11. To *record* problem-solving techniques.
12. To *keep track* of the number of problems solved, books read, or homework assignments completed.

Brownlie, Close, and Wingren (1990) and Fogarty and Bellanca (1987) identify certain prompts or lead-ins that promote thinking at higher levels. Brownlie et al. suggest teachers use prompts at the beginning, middle, and end of a lesson, and to comment on the group process.

Some examples of prompts or lead-ins are as follows:

To Begin
- What questions do you have from yesterday?
- Write two important points from yesterday's lesson.

In the Middle
- What do you want to know more about?
- How is this like something else?
- Is this easy or hard for you? Explain why.

At the End
- Something I heard that surprised me…
- How will you use this outside of class?

On the Group Process
- I helped move my group's thinking forward because…
- The group helped my thinking because…
- An example of collaboration today was…

Fogarty and Bellanca (1987) suggest lead-ins for logging that encourage responses that are analytical, synthetic, and evaluative. Examples of log stems include:

One thing I'm excited about is…because…
I hate it when…because…
This is like a movie I saw…because…

PAUSE

Fogarty and Bellanca (1987) suggest lead-ins for logging that encourage responses that are analytical, synthetic, and evaluative.

HOW SHOULD WE USE LEARNING LOGS AND JOURNALS?

Learning logs and journals are usually considered formative methods of assessment that can be assigned numerical or letter grades or point values. The following methods of assessment may be helpful:

1. Jeroski, Brownlie, and Kaser, (1990b) developed indicators to describe the depth and personalization of students' responses to their readings. They scored sixth grade students' responses to a poem using the following criteria: powerful, competent, partial, and undeveloped.

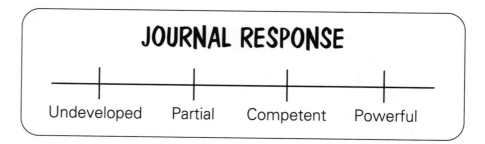

JOURNAL RESPONSE

Undeveloped   Partial   Competent   Powerful

2. Another way to assess journal responses is by the level of thoughtfulness: little evidence, some evidence, and strong evidence.

JOURNAL RESPONSE

Little Evidence of Thoughtfulness	Some Evidence of Thoughtfulness	Strong Evidence of Thoughtfulness
Response only	Response supported by specific examples	Response supported by examples and personal reflections

PAUSE

Learning logs and journals are usually considered formative methods of assessment that can be assigned numerical or letter grades or point values.

88

3. Teachers can assign point values for logs or journals:

   <u>20</u> points for completing all logs or journals
   <u>10</u> points for completing all logs or journals on time
   <u>15</u> points for originality of ideas
   <u>15</u> points for evidence of higher-order thinking
   <u>15</u> points for making connections
   <u>25</u> points for personal reflection

   <u>100</u> total points

4. Sample criteria and indicators can be used to assess logs and journals on a Likert scale that measures growth on a continuum.
   • descriptive words
   • number of entries
   • length of response
   • use of concrete images
   • dialogue
   • connections to other subjects
   • thoughtfulness
   • originality
   • creativity

PAUSE

Sample criteria and indicators can be used to assess logs and journals on a Likert scale that measures growth on a continuum.

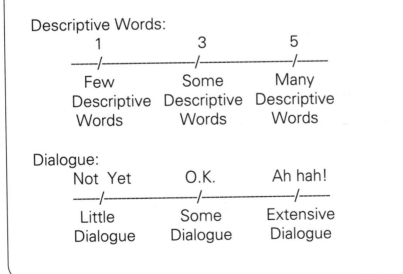

JOURNAL ENTRIES

Descriptive Words:

1	3	5
Few Descriptive Words	Some Descriptive Words	Many Descriptive Words

Dialogue:

Not Yet	O.K.	Ah hah!
Little Dialogue	Some Dialogue	Extensive Dialogue

5. Students can turn in journals on a periodic basis for feedback and/or a grade. The grade can be based on the number of entries, the quality of entries (based on predetermined criteria), or a combination of quantity and quality.

6. Students can share journal entries with a buddy or a cooperative group. Peers may provide both oral and written feedback based on predetermined criteria and assign a grade.

7. Students complete a self-assessment on their journal entries based on predetermined criteria.

8. Students and/or teachers can select a few of the journal entries to be rewritten and turned in for a grade or be placed in the portfolio.

PAUSE

Students and/or teachers can select a few of the journal entries to be rewritten and turned in for a grade or be placed in the portfolio.

Students can respond in their journal to the following:

1) Magazine & Newspaper Articles
2) Literature
3) Independent Reading
4) Videos
5) Guest Speaker
6) Field trip
7) Assemblies
8) Personal feelings or memories
9) Others

EXAMPLES

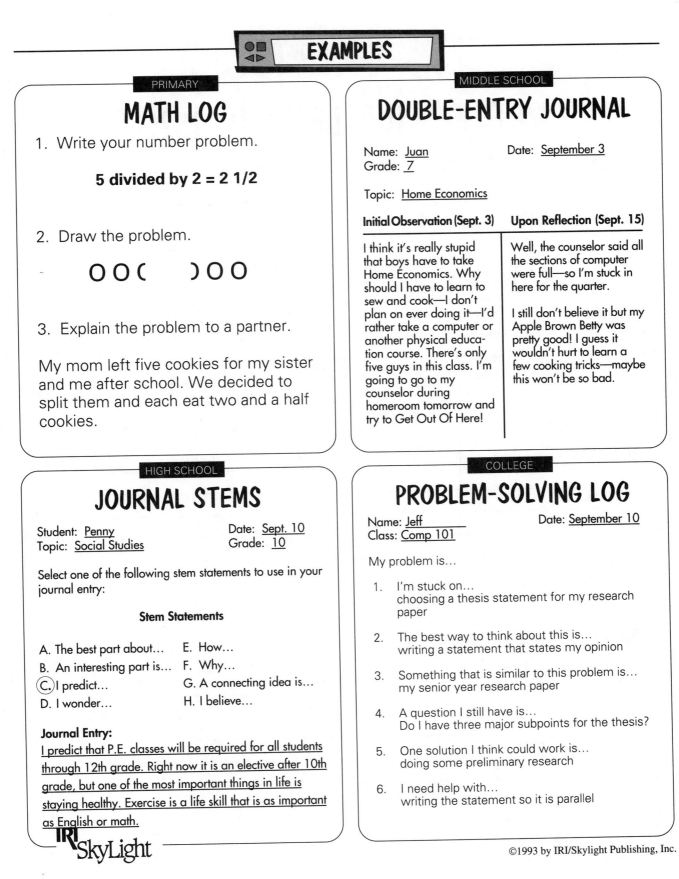

PRIMARY
MATH LOG

1. Write your number problem.

   5 divided by 2 = 2 1/2

2. Draw the problem.

   O O O   O O O

3. Explain the problem to a partner.

My mom left five cookies for my sister and me after school. We decided to split them and each eat two and a half cookies.

MIDDLE SCHOOL
DOUBLE-ENTRY JOURNAL

Name: Juan   Date: September 3
Grade: 7

Topic: Home Economics

Initial Observation (Sept. 3)	Upon Reflection (Sept. 15)
I think it's really stupid that boys have to take Home Economics. Why should I have to learn to sew and cook—I don't plan on ever doing it—I'd rather take a computer or another physical education course. There's only five guys in this class. I'm going to go to my counselor during homeroom tomorrow and try to Get Out Of Here!	Well, the counselor said all the sections of computer were full—so I'm stuck in here for the quarter. I still don't believe it but my Apple Brown Betty was pretty good! I guess it wouldn't hurt to learn a few cooking tricks—maybe this won't be so bad.

HIGH SCHOOL
JOURNAL STEMS

Student: Penny   Date: Sept. 10
Topic: Social Studies   Grade: 10

Select one of the following stem statements to use in your journal entry:

Stem Statements

A. The best part about...   E. How...
B. An interesting part is... F. Why...
C. I predict...   G. A connecting idea is...
D. I wonder...   H. I believe...

Journal Entry:

I predict that P.E. classes will be required for all students through 12th grade. Right now it is an elective after 10th grade, but one of the most important things in life is staying healthy. Exercise is a life skill that is as important as English or math.

COLLEGE
PROBLEM-SOLVING LOG

Name: Jeff   Date: September 10
Class: Comp 101

My problem is...

1. I'm stuck on...
   choosing a thesis statement for my research paper

2. The best way to think about this is...
   writing a statement that states my opinion

3. Something that is similar to this problem is...
   my senior year research paper

4. A question I still have is...
   Do I have three major subpoints for the thesis?

5. One solution I think could work is...
   doing some preliminary research

6. I need help with...
   writing the statement so it is parallel

IRI SkyLight

ON YOUR OWN

REFLECTIVE LESSON LOG

Directions: Try using this log with your students during a lecture.

Name: _____   Date: _____

Topic: _____

1. Key ideas from this discussion _____
    _____
    _____
    _____
    _____
    _____
    _____
    _____

2. Connections I can make with other ideas _____
    _____
    _____
    _____
    _____
    _____
    _____

3. Questions I still have _____
    _____
    _____
    _____
    _____
    _____
    _____
    _____

IRI SkyLight

⊞ ON YOUR OWN

JOURNAL STEMS

1. Create some original stem statements that would motivate your students to write in their logs or journals.

    Example: My worst nightmare is…

    Stem Statements

    -
    -
    -

    -
    -
    -

2. Create a log or journal idea that would help your students retain key ideas, process information, connect ideas, or reflect on their learnings.

1. when I hear the word journal I…
2. Students need to write more because
3. I need to "chunk" my lectures because…
4. I predict   5. Your choice…

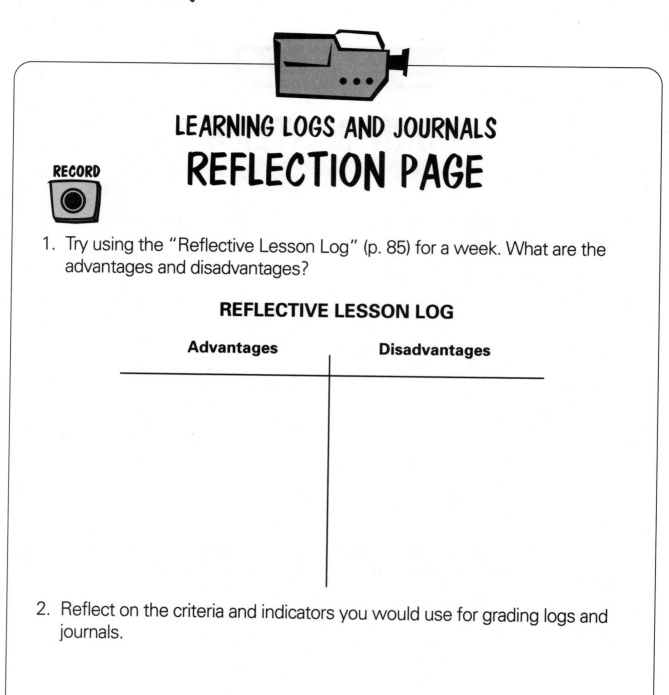

LEARNING LOGS AND JOURNALS
REFLECTION PAGE

RECORD

1. Try using the "Reflective Lesson Log" (p. 85) for a week. What are the advantages and disadvantages?

REFLECTIVE LESSON LOG

Advantages	Disadvantages

2. Reflect on the criteria and indicators you would use for grading logs and journals.

3. Think about how logs and journals could be included in a portfolio. How many would you include? Who should select them? Would they be graded? Would peers read them and make comments?

IRI SkyLight

METACOGNITIVE REFLECTION

CHAPTER 8

"Some people are unaware of their own thinking processes while they are thinking. When asked, 'How are you solving that problem?' they may reply, 'I don't know, I'm just doing it.' They can't describe the steps and sequences that they use before, during, or after problem solving."

-Costa, 1991, p. 23

WHAT IS METACOGNITIVE REFLECTION?

PAUSE

"Thinking involves not only cognitive operations but the dispositions to engage in them when and where appropriate."
-Barell, 1992, p. 259

Swartz and Perkins define metacognition as "becoming aware of your thought processes in order to then control them when appropriate" (as cited in Barell, 1992, p. 258). Barell (1992) states that researchers and practitioners usually focus primarily on the cognitive when discussing metacognition because that is part of the definition: "along" or "beyond" one's cognitive operations.

But Barell argues that feelings, attitudes, and dispositions play a vital role in metacognition since *"thinking* involves not only cognitive operations but the dispositions to engage in them when and where appropriate" (Barell, 1992, p. 259).

Metacognitive reflections allow students to manage and assess their own thinking strategies. "Metacognition involves the monitoring and control of attitudes, such as students' beliefs about themselves, the value of persistence, the nature of work, and their personal responsibility in accomplishing a goal" (Fusco & Fountain, 1992, p. 240). These attitudes are essential components in all tasks—academic and nonacademic.

All teachers need to introduce strategies that promote metacognition. Moreover, students need to self-reflect regularly so that they can become adept at monitoring, assessing, and improving their own performances and their own thinking.

One of the key pieces in the portrait of a student involves self-assessment. In teachers' attempt to "cover the content," "teach the textbook," and "prepare students for the test," they often neglect the critical piece that allows everyone to step back and reflect on "what we did well, what we would do differently, and whether or not we need help." Individual students, cooperative groups, and teachers need to take the time to process what they have done and to internalize metacognitive strategies.

WHY SHOULD WE USE METACOGNITIVE REFLECTION?

Perkins and Salomon (1992), and Fogarty, Perkins, and Barell (1992) all describe the critical relationships between metacognition and transfer. "In order to transfer knowledge or skills from one situation to another, we must be aware of them; metacognitive strategies are designed to help students become more aware" (Barell, 1992, p. 259).

Educators used to think that students will automatically take what teachers teach and apply or transfer it to other places or areas. Yet, students often do not connect what they learned in English to social studies, or what they learned in math class to a mathematical problem they encounter at work or in life. Transfer plays a key role in metacognition.

Fogarty, Perkins, and Barell (1992) define transfer as "learning something in one context and applying it in another" (p. ix). They give examples of how people can learn to drive a car (the first context), and then later when they have to rent a small truck, they can drive it fairly well (the second context). Or when one learns a foreign language like French, some of the vocabulary can carry over to Italian.

It is evident that transfer does not happen automatically unless teachers teach for it. Journals, thoughtful questioning, goal setting, problem-based learning, and self-assessments can help make students become more aware of their thought processes and, therefore, more able to transfer those strategies to real-life situations.

"Ordinary learning contrasts with transfer. In ordinary learning, we just do more of the same thing in the same situations…. Real transfer happens when people carry over something they learned in one context to a 'significantly different' context" (Fogarty, Perkins, and Barell, 1992, p. ix). Fogarty et al. (1992) use the following graphic to illustrate the situational dispositions for transfer. They use six birds to represent the different models.

PAUSE

"In order to transfer knowledge or skills from one situation to another, we must be aware of them; metacognitive strategies are designed to help students become more aware."
-Barell, 1992, p. 259

Thinking *Metacognition* *about Thinking*

How to Assess Authentic Learning

Transfer
Taking something you learned
+ applying to new situation

SITUATIONAL DISPOSITIONS FOR TRANSFER

Model	Illustration	Transfer Disposition	Looks Like	Sounds Like
BIRDS Ollie the Head-in-the-Sand Ostrich	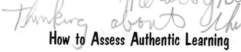	*Overlooks*	Persists in writing in manuscript form rather than cursive. (New skill overlooked or avoided.)	*"I get it right on the dittos, but I forget to use punctuation when I write an essay."* (Not applying mechanical learning.)
Dan the Drilling Woodpecker		*Duplicates*	Plagiarism is the most obvious student artifact of duplication. (Unable to synthesize in own words.)	*"Mine is not to question why—just invert and multiply."* [When dividing fractions.] (No understanding of what he or she is doing.)
Laura the Look-Alike Penguin		*Replicates*	"Bed to Bed" or narrative style. "He got up. He did this. He went to bed." or "He was born. He did this. He died." (Student portfolio of work never varies.)	*"Paragraphing means I must have three 'indents' per page."* (Tailors into own story or essay, but paragraphs inappropriately.)
Jonathan Livingston Seagull		*Integrates*	Student writing essay incorporates newly learned French words. (Applying: weaving old and new.)	*"I always try to guess (predict) what's going to happen next on T.V. shows."* (Connects to prior knowledge and experience; relates what's learned to personal experience.)
Cathy the Carrier Pigeon		*Maps*	Graphs information for a social studies report with the help of the math teacher to actually design the graphs. (Connecting to another.)	From a parent: *"Tina suggested we brainstorm our vacation ideas and rank them to help us decide."* (Carries new skills into life situations.)
Samantha the Soaring Eagle		*Innovates*	After studying flow charts for computer class, student constructs a Rube Goldberg-type invention. (Innovates; diverges; goes beyond and creates novelty.)	*"I took the idea of the Mr. Potato Head and created a mix-and-match grid of ideas for our Earth Day project."* (Generalizes ideas from experience and transfers creatively.)

Reprinted with permission from *The Mindful School: How to Teach for Transfer* (1992) by Fogarty, Perkins, and Barell.

HOW SHOULD WE USE METACOGNITIVE REFLECTION?

Teachers can use journals as metacognitive strategies by assessing the reflectiveness of the students' responses, the evidence of transfer to other classes or life outside school, and the students' ability to plan, monitor, and evaluate their own work.

Bellanca and Fogarty suggest a series of questions called Mrs. Potter's Questions to help individuals and groups process and reflect on their individual work or their group work.

1. What were you expected to do?
2. In this assignment, what did you do well?
3. If you had to do this task over, what would you do differently?
4. What help do you need from me? (Fogarty & Bellanca, 1987, p. 227)

Teachers can monitor students' use of metacognition and assess it, if necessary, by checking the students' work to look for some of the following:

1. The number of metacognitive strategies used by the student.
2. Evidence of reflection in written and oral work.

```
/——————————/——————————/
Little            Some              Much
Evidence          Evidence          Evidence
```

3. Ability to connect one idea to another in written or oral work.
4. Ability to transfer an idea from one class to another class or to a situation outside of school.
5. Quality and depth of the responses.
6. Ability to brainstorm or generate ideas.
7. Ability to evaluate one's own work and the work of others.
8. Ability to solve problems and to make decisions.

PAUSE

Teachers can use journals as metacognitive strategies by assessing the reflectiveness of the students' responses, the evidence of transfer to other classes or life outside school, and the students' ability to plan, monitor, and evaluate their own work.

How to Assess Authentic Learning

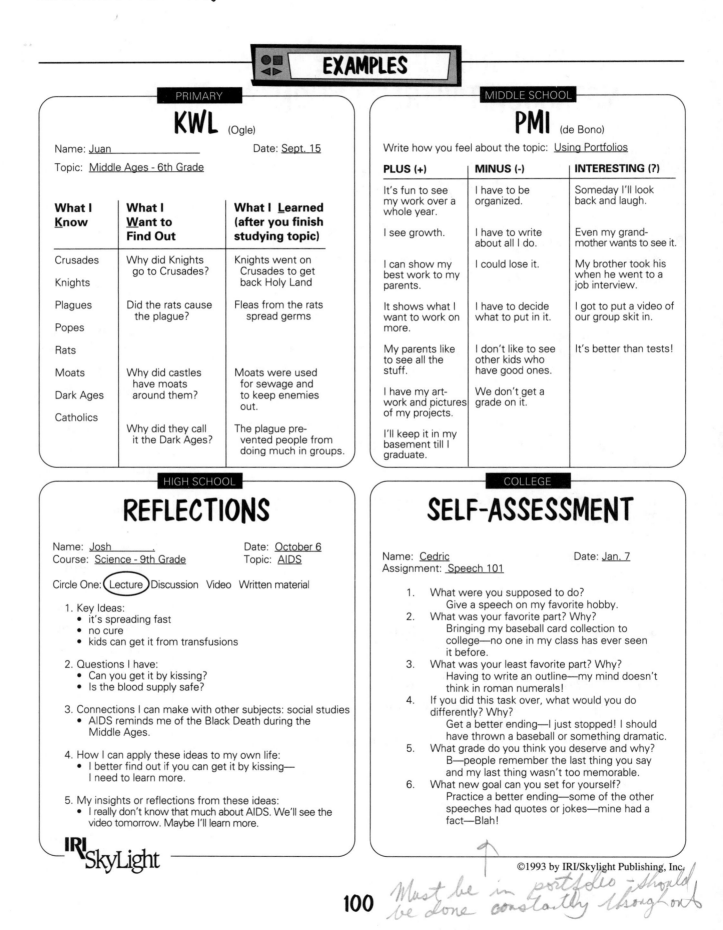

EXAMPLES

PRIMARY

KWL (Ogle)

Name: Juan   Date: Sept. 15

Topic: Middle Ages - 6th Grade

What I Know	What I Want to Find Out	What I Learned (after you finish studying topic)
Crusades	Why did Knights go to Crusades?	Knights went on Crusades to get back Holy Land
Knights		
Plagues	Did the rats cause the plague?	Fleas from the rats spread germs
Popes		
Rats		
Moats	Why did castles have moats around them?	Moats were used for sewage and to keep enemies out.
Dark Ages		
Catholics		
	Why did they call it the Dark Ages?	The plague prevented people from doing much in groups.

MIDDLE SCHOOL

PMI (de Bono)

Write how you feel about the topic: Using Portfolios

PLUS (+)	MINUS (-)	INTERESTING (?)
It's fun to see my work over a whole year.	I have to be organized.	Someday I'll look back and laugh.
I see growth.	I have to write about all I do.	Even my grandmother wants to see it.
I can show my best work to my parents.	I could lose it.	My brother took his when he went to a job interview.
It shows what I want to work on more.	I have to decide what to put in it.	I got to put a video of our group skit in.
My parents like to see all the stuff.	I don't like to see other kids who have good ones.	It's better than tests!
I have my artwork and pictures of my projects.	We don't get a grade on it.	
I'll keep it in my basement till I graduate.		

HIGH SCHOOL

REFLECTIONS

Name: Josh   Date: October 6
Course: Science - 9th Grade   Topic: AIDS

Circle One: (Lecture) Discussion Video Written material

1. Key Ideas:
   • it's spreading fast
   • no cure
   • kids can get it from transfusions

2. Questions I have:
   • Can you get it by kissing?
   • Is the blood supply safe?

3. Connections I can make with other subjects: social studies
   • AIDS reminds me of the Black Death during the Middle Ages.

4. How I can apply these ideas to my own life:
   • I better find out if you can get it by kissing—I need to learn more.

5. My insights or reflections from these ideas:
   • I really don't know that much about AIDS. We'll see the video tomorrow. Maybe I'll learn more.

COLLEGE

SELF-ASSESSMENT

Name: Cedric   Date: Jan. 7
Assignment: Speech 101

1. What were you supposed to do?
   Give a speech on my favorite hobby.
2. What was your favorite part? Why?
   Bringing my baseball card collection to college—no one in my class has ever seen it before.
3. What was your least favorite part? Why?
   Having to write an outline—my mind doesn't think in roman numerals!
4. If you did this task over, what would you do differently? Why?
   Get a better ending—I just stopped! I should have thrown a baseball or something dramatic.
5. What grade do you think you deserve and why?
   B—people remember the last thing you say and my last thing wasn't too memorable.
6. What new goal can you set for yourself?
   Practice a better ending—some of the other speeches had quotes or jokes—mine had a fact—Blah!

IRI SkyLight

Must be in portfolio - should be done constantly throughout

ON YOUR OWN

SELF-ASSESSMENT

Create an original self-assessment tool your students can use for an individual project, group project, performance, or portfolio.

IRI SkyLight

ON YOUR OWN

WRAP-AROUND

The "wrap-around" is an effective reflective piece that teachers can use in the middle or at the end of a lesson to find out how students feel and what they remember about a lesson. Write a few stem statements on the board and divide the room so that each student knows what stem question they will answer. Give enough wait-time to allow everyone time to reflect. Go around the room and call on each student to complete the stem statement assigned:

SAMPLE WRAP-AROUND STEMS:

One thing I learned is…
The thing that really surprised me is…
One thing I'll remember 25 years from now is…
If I had taught this lesson, I would have…

Create your own wrap-around stems to use with your class.

WRAP-AROUND STEMS

Stem: _____

Stem: _____

Stem: _____

Stem: _____

Ask your students to help create their own stems.

IRI SkyLight

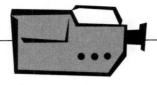

METACOGNITIVE REFLECTION
REFLECTION PAGE

"We must constantly remind ourselves that the ultimate purpose of evaluation is to have students become self-evaluating" (Costa & Kallick, 1992, p. 280). Comment on this statement and reflect on how you can incorporate more metacognitive activities and self-assessments in your teaching.

_____

_____

_____

_____

_____

_____

_____

_____

_____

_____

_____

_____

_____

_____

_____

_____

_____

_____

_____

_____

_____

IRI
SkyLight

Notes:

_____
_____
_____
_____
_____
_____
_____
_____
_____
_____
_____
_____
_____
_____
_____
_____
_____
_____
_____
_____
_____
_____
_____
_____
_____
_____
_____

OBSERVATION CHECKLISTS

CHAPTER 9

"Assessing thinking skills with a paper-and-pencil test places our students in untenable situations, but there is a technique teachers can use to measure thinking skills. It isn't perfect, but it seems fairer and more reliable than paper-and-pencil tests— observation."

- Rhoades & McCabe, 1992, p. 50

WHAT ARE OBSERVATION CHECKLISTS?

The observation checklist is a strategy to monitor specific skills, behaviors, or dispositions of individual students or all of the students in the class. It is also a record-keeping device for teachers to use to keep track of who has mastered the targeted skills and who still needs help. Effective checklists include students' names, space for four to five targeted areas, a code or rating to determine to what degree the student has or has not demonstrated the skill (**+** = frequently; ✓ = sometimes; ○ = not yet!), and a space for comments or anecdotal notes. Some teachers find it useful to date the occurrences so they can see developmental growth or use the checklists for both student and parent conferences.

Teachers can use observation checklists for formative assessments by focusing on specific behaviors, thinking, social skills, writing skills, speaking skills, or athletic skills. Peers can use checklists to assess the progress of another student; cooperative group members can monitor the entire group's progress. These checklists can then be shared and discussed among group members to determine who needs additional help in different areas and how the whole group is performing overall.

With the increased emphasis on self-reflection and self-assessment, individual students should use self-checklists to assess their own progress and to develop an improvement plan.

PAUSE

Peers can use checklists to assess the progress of another student; cooperative group members can monitor the entire group's progress.

WHY SHOULD WE USE OBSERVATION CHECKLISTS?

The checklist provides a quick and easy way to observe and record many of the skills and behaviors that are rarely assessed prior to the final test or summative evaluation. Too often, teachers do not realize a student needs help until it is too late. Checklists show teachers and students the areas that need work early enough to be able to help the student before he or she fails the test or the unit. They also provide the opportunity to "change gears" in a classroom if a large percentage of the students are not doing well.

Costa (1991) recommends that characteristics of intelligent behavior such as persistence, listening, flexibility in thinking, metacognition, and checking for accuracy and precision can be taught and observed by students, parents, and teachers. Observation checklists are tools to use to check off whether or not the student can demonstrate the skill or attribute being measured. Observation checklists also focus on observable performances or criteria that are often more meaningful or authentic than paper-and-pencil tests. By focusing on two or three concrete skills or criteria, teachers and students can monitor growth or need for improvement more easily.

Observation is one of the most effective tools to find out what children can do and what their learning needs are. In a resource guide for parents and teachers that discusses how to assess the progress of primary-age children, the Ministry of Education in British Columbia recommends that teachers watch children throughout the year and "record observations of children in action and review them on a regular basis to discover patterns, assess progress and make plans to help children continue their learning" (Ministry of Education, Province of B.C., 1991, Supporting Learning, p. 14). The Ministry recommends that teachers structure tasks to develop a base of information about each child and use the checklist to chart progress over time.

Teachers and parents can observe children in a variety of settings:

- classrooms
- playground
- field trips
- hallways
- gym

- individually
- in groups (pairs, small or large groups)
- with younger children
- with older children
- with adults

It is possible to observe children perform a variety of tasks:

- reading
- writing
- computing
- problem solving
- singing
- working

- constructing
- talking
- map making
- classifying
- listening
- sorting
- playing music

- dancing
- playing
- building
- drawing
- painting
- typing
- miming

PAUSE

Observation checklists also focus on observable performances or criteria that are often more meaningful or authentic than paper-and-pencil tests.

107

- graphing
- socializing
- dramatizing
- word processing

(Ministry of Education, Province of British Columbia, 1991, Supporting Learning, p. 14)

By observing children and charting their progress on notecards, observation checklists, Post-it notes put in files, or portfolios, teachers can learn about students' learning styles, learning needs, attitudes, initiative, likes and dislikes, and need for assistance (Ministry of Education, Province of British Columbia, Supporting Learning, 1991).

PAUSE

⏸

Students should be trained in what the skill "looks like" and "sounds like" if they are going to be asked to observe their peers or perform a self-assessment.

HOW SHOULD WE USE OBSERVATION CHECKLISTS?

Each teacher can determine which specific areas to include in the observation checklist and then make sure the students are aware of the areas that will be observed. Students should be trained in what the skill "looks like" and "sounds like" if they are going to be asked to observe their peers or perform a self-assessment. It is imperative that the skills and processes being observed are modeled and taught to the students prior to the observations.

For example, if students are going to be observed on persistence, they should work with the teacher to list observable indicators of persistence:

Criterion—"Persistence"	Observed Frequently	Observed Sometimes	Not Yet Observed
Indicators:			
1. knows how to access information			
2. tries several approaches			
3. does not give up quickly			
4. has patience			
5. brainstorms alternative solutions			
6. checks own work			

Another way teachers can work with students to identify key characteristics or indicators of observable skills, attitudes, dispositions, behaviors, or processes is to develop a graphic organizer called a T-chart. A T-chart helps students understand what certain behaviors "look like" and "sound like." For example, if a teacher is observing the social skill "encouragement," the entire class can complete a T-chart prior to the observation.

ENCOURAGEMENT

What does it look like?	What does it sound like?
1. Looking at the person who is talking.	1. "I like that idea."
2. Nodding your head.	2. "Tell me more."
3. Patting the person on the back.	3. "What do you think?"
4. Using a sign like "thumbs-up" or "high-five."	4. "Good job."
5. Applauding appropriately.	5. "We really want your opinion."

HOW TO USE OBSERVATION CHECKLISTS

The following ideas can be incorporated into observation checklists that teachers can use to monitor and document students' skills, processes, and behaviors.

WRITING PROCESSES

GRAMMAR AND USAGE
Sentence structure
Subject-verb
    agreement
Comma splices
Plurals of nouns
Pronouns/Agreement
Verb tenses
Use of adjectives
Use of adverbs
Fragments
Run-on sentences

MECHANICS
Capital letters
Commas
Semicolons
Colons
Question marks

Apostrophes
Spelling

ORGANIZATION
Outline
Introduction
Topic sentences
Support sentences
Transitions
Conclusion

RESEARCH SKILLS
Selection of topic
Review of literature
Working bibliography
Thesis statement
Outline
Paraphrasing
Documentation
Final bibliography
Proofreading

OTHER PROCESSES

MULTIPLE INTELLIGENCES
Verbal/Linguistic
Logical/Mathematical
Visual/Spatial
Musical/Rhythmic
Bodily/Kinesthetic
Interpersonal
Intrapersonal

SPEAKING SKILLS
Eye contact
Facial expression
Voice inflection
Enthusiasm
Organization
Use of facts
Visual aids
Movement
Persuasiveness

Body language
Gestures

ART LAB
Creativity
Originality
Use of multiple media
Color sense

ORAL READING
Pronunciation
Enunciation
Expression
Fluency

SOCIAL SKILLS

FORMATION OF GROUPS
Forms groups quietly
Sits eyeball to eyeball
Makes eye contact
Uses first names
Shares materials
Follows role
    assignments

SUPPORT
Checks for
    understanding
Offers help
Asks the group for help
Encourages others
Energizes the group
Disagrees with the
    idea—not the person

COMMUNICATION
Uses low voices
Takes turns
Makes sure everyone
    speaks
Waits until speaker is
    finished before
    speaking

CONFLICT RESOLUTION
Disagrees with the
    idea—not the person
Respects the opinion
    of others
Thinks for self
Explores different
    points of view
Negotiates and/or
    compromises
Reaches consensus

THINKING PROCESSES

CRITICAL THINKING SKILLS
Analyzing for bias
Attributing
Cause and effect
Classifying
Comparing
Inferring
Contrasting
Decision making
Drawing conclusions
Evaluating
Prioritizing

Sequencing
Solving analogies

CREATIVE THINKING SKILLS
Brainstorming
Generalizing
Hypothesizing
Inventing
Making analogies
Paradox
Personifying
Predicting
Problem solving

INTELLIGENT BEHAVIORS

Persistence
Listening
Flexibility in thinking

Metacognition
Checking for accuracy
Precision

IRI/SkyLight

EXAMPLES

PRIMARY

SOCIAL SKILLS CHECKLIST

ASSESSMENT OF SOCIAL SKILLS

Dates: 10/21
Class: 3rd Grade
Teacher: Forbes
Ratings:
+ = Frequently
✓ = Sometimes
○ = Not Yet

Who	Listening Skill 1	Using First Names Skill 2	Taking Turns Skill 3	Encouraging Skill 4	Sharing Skill 5	Celebrations
1. Lois	✓	✓	○	✓	✓	
2. Connie	+	+	○	✓	+	Dropped in 2 areas
3. James	✓	✓	✓	✓	✓	
4. Juan	+	+	✓	+	+	
5. Beth	○	○	+	✓	✓	Improved in 2 areas
6. Michele	✓	✓	○	✓	✓	
7. John	✓	✓	○	✓	✓	
8. Charles	+	+	○	✓	+	
9. Mike	✓	✓	✓	✓	✓	Went from 5 O's to this in 2 months
10. Lana	+	+	✓	+	+	

COMMENTS: Work with Lois on a regular basis. Change her seat and group.

MIDDLE SCHOOL

OBSERVATION CHECKLIST

Student ___Denise___ Class ___Science___ Date 12/5
Type of Assignment: Work Habits

☐ Teacher   Date _____ Signed _____
☐ Peer   Date _____ Signed _____
☒ Self   Date 12/5   Signed *Denise Smith*

	Frequently	Sometimes	Not Yet
WORK HABITS:			
• Gets work done on time	X		
• Asks for help when needed		X	
• Takes initiative		X	
STUDY HABITS:			
• Organizes work	X		
• Takes good notes	X		
• Uses time well	X		
PERSISTENCE:			
• Shows patience		X	
• Checks own work			X
• Revises work		X	
• Does quality work	X		
SOCIAL SKILLS:			
• Works well with others		X	
• Listens to others		X	
• Helps others		X	

COMMENTS: I always get my work done on time, and I am really organized. I just need to check my own work and help my group work. Future goal: I need to be more patient with my group and try to work with them more. I worry about my own grades, but I don't do enough to help them achieve their goals.

HIGH SCHOOL

BASKETBALL SKILLS

Teacher: Ms. Moss   Class: 5th Period P.E.   Date: 11/22
Target Skills: Students will develop basketball skills and teamwork

Ratings:
+ = Frequently
✓ = Sometimes
○ = Not Yet

STUDENTS DEMONSTRATE THE FOLLOWING

NAMES OF STUDENTS	Dribbling Skills	Passing Skills	Free Throw Skills	Team Spirit	Sportsmanship	COMMENTS
1. Toni	✓	+	○	○	✓	
2. Casey	+	+	○	✓	+	
3. James	✓	✓	○	✓	✓	
4. Juan	+	+	✓	+	+	Real potential
5. Beth	✓	✓	✓	✓	✓	
6. Michael	✓	✓	○	✓	✓	Practice free throws
7. Judy	+	○	✓	+	+	
8. Charles	○	○	+	✓	✓	Does not like team sports
9. Dave	✓	+	○	✓	+	
10. Lisa	+	+	✓	+	+	Excellent player

COLLEGE

WRITING CHECKLIST

Key:
+ = Good
✓ = OK
○ = Not Yet

☐ Teacher
☐ Peer
☒ Self

Student: Robin   Class: English 102
Paper Teaching for Transfer

	Date: 9/1	Date: 11/5	Date: 1/2
Usage			
1. Topic Sentence	+	+	+
2. Complete Sentences	+	+	+
3. Complex Sentences	○	○	○
4. Wide Vocabulary	○	✓	+
Mechanics			
5. Capitalization	+	+	+
6. Punctuation	✓	✓	✓
7. Spelling	○	✓	+
8. Grammar	✓	✓	+

Strengths: My topic sentences, sentence structure, and capitalization are good.

Not Yet: I need to write more complex sentences - most of my sentences are simple.

IRI SkyLight

T-CHART GRAPHIC ORGANIZER

The T-chart is a graphic organizer that helps teachers and students focus on the specific behaviors that can be observed. For example:

SKILL: <u>Intelligent behavior—checking for accuracy</u>

What does it look like?	What does it sound like?
Using spell check Using a dictionary Checking sources Having a peer read material Proofreading carefully Reading out loud Using calculator	"How do you spell 'receive'?" "Where is our grammar reference book?" "Give me the thesaurus." "Will you edit this for me?" "Let me check my figures again." "This is my third draft."

Select one social skill, thinking process, or intelligent behavior and complete a T-chart with your class.

SKILL: _____

What does it look like?	What does it sound like?

◖▣◗ ON YOUR OWN

Directions: Select the skills you want to observe and write them on the five slanted lines at the top.

OBSERVATION CHECKLIST

Teacher: _____ Class:_____ Date:_____

Target Skills: _____

Ratings:
+ = Frequently
✓ = Sometimes
○ = Not Yet

NAMES OF STUDENTS						COMMENTS
1.						
2.						
3.						
4.						
5.						
6.						
7.						
8.						
9.						
10.						
11.						
12.						
13.						
14.						
15.						
16.						
17.						
18.						
19						

IRI SkyLight

BONUS

INDIVIDUAL OBSERVATION CHECKLIST

Directions: Select criteria you want to observe and list specific indicators that describe those criteria (see Middle School Example, p. 111).

Student: _____ Class: _____ Date: _____

Type of Assignment: _____

☐ Teacher   Date _____ Signed _____

☐ Peer   Date _____ Signed _____

☐ Self   Date _____ Signed _____

	Frequently	Sometimes	Not Yet
_____			
• _____	_____	_____	_____
• _____	_____	_____	_____
• _____	_____	_____	_____
• _____	_____	_____	_____
_____			
• _____	_____	_____	_____
• _____	_____	_____	_____
• _____	_____	_____	_____
• _____	_____	_____	_____
_____			
• _____	_____	_____	_____
• _____	_____	_____	_____
• _____	_____	_____	_____
• _____	_____	_____	_____
_____			
• _____	_____	_____	_____
• _____	_____	_____	_____
• _____	_____	_____	_____
• _____	_____	_____	_____

COMMENTS: _____

_____

_____

IRI SkyLight

BONUS

Directions: Ask each member of the group to tally the number of times they see other group members using the targeted social skill.

GROUP OBSERVATION CHECKLIST

Topic: _____Date: _____

Class: _____ Teacher:_____

DIRECTIONS:

1.   Select a social skill you plan to observe for one activity, one day, or one week.

2.   Put a "✓" every time you observe your team members use the social skill.

3.   Fill in the comments section below.

4.   Share your observations and comments with your group members.

GROUP MEMBERS	TARGETED SOCIAL SKILL	MON.	TUES.	WED.	THURS.	FRI.	TOTAL
1.							
2.							
3.							
4.							

COMMENTS: _____

_____

_____

_____

_____

Signed: _____   Date: _____

©1993 by IRI/Skylight Publishing, Inc.

OBSERVATION CHECKLISTS
REFLECTION PAGE

RECORD

1. How can students become more involved in monitoring their group members and themselves?

_____

_____

_____

_____

_____

_____

_____

_____

2. Reflect on how observation checklists completed by the teacher, peers, or individuals are valuable formative assessments.

_____

_____

_____

_____

_____

_____

_____

_____

IRI SkyLight

GRAPHIC ORGANIZERS

CHAPTER **10**

"Graphic organizers embedded in a cooperative environment are more powerful teaching tools than teacher talk or conventional skill drill techniques. The graphic organizers are also tools for more sophisticated and authentic assessment approaches."

-Bellanca, 1992a, p. vi

WHAT ARE GRAPHIC ORGANIZERS?

PAUSE

Graphic organizers such as the web, Venn, concept map, and many others help students make their thinking visible.

Graphic organizers are mental maps that represent key skills like sequencing, comparing and contrasting, and classifying and involve students in active thinking. These mental maps depict complex relationships and promote clearer understanding of content lessons (Black & Black, 1990). "Once the content priorities are established, the strategic teacher can focus on identifying organizational patterns that will help frame student thinking about the content and will influence considerations about the criterial task" (Jones, Palincsar, Ogle, and Carr, 1987, p. 37).

Graphic organizers serve as effective tools for helping both teachers and students do the following:

1. represent abstract or implicit information in a more concrete form,
2. depict relationships between facts and concepts,
3. generate and organize ideas for writing,
4. relate new information to prior knowledge,
5. store and retrieve information, and
6. assess student thinking and learning.

(McTighe & Lyman, 1992, p. 81)

Graphic organizers such as the web (Hawley), Venn diagram (Venn), concept map (Rico, Buzan), and many others help students make their thinking visible. They also "become a metacognitive tool to transfer the thinking processes to other lessons which feature the same relationships" (Black & Black, 1990, p. 2).

Teachers at all grade levels can introduce thinking skills by drawing a web on the blackboard and asking students to brainstorm characteristics or attributes of a topic, such as "baseball." By using a Venn diagram, students can compare and contrast baseball and football. And by using a mind map, students can brainstorm all types of sports and classify them into clusters. Each graphic organizer helps students reinforce one or more specific thinking skills.

Teachers can do the following when introducing new graphic organizers:

1. Introduce the new organizer and model how to use it with the whole class by selecting a topic that is easily understood by all of the students.
2. Allow students to practice using the graphic organizer in small groups. Let them select a topic of their choice.
3. Ask individual students to complete a graphic organizer on their own in class or for homework.
4. Encourage students or groups to create an original organizer to share subject content with the class.

WHY SHOULD WE USE GRAPHIC ORGANIZERS?

Many students cannot connect or relate new information to prior knowledge because they have trouble remembering things. Graphic organizers can help them remember because they become "blueprints" or maps that make abstract ideas more visible and concrete. Students also need to make connections between prior knowledge, what they are doing today, and what they can apply or transfer to other things. Graphic organizers can help bridge those connections and make them stronger. Students who are visual learners *need* graphic organizers to help them organize information and remember key concepts.

Jones, Palincsar, Ogle, & Carr say that "graphic organizers and graphic outlining systems with frames and procedures for summarizing can be powerful tools to help students locate, select, sequence, integrate, and restructure information—both from the perspective of understanding and from the perspective of producing information in written responses" (1987, p. 38).

PAUSE

Students who are visual learners *need* graphic organizers to help them organize information and remember key concepts.

HOW SHOULD WE ASSESS GRAPHIC ORGANIZERS?

PAUSE

Including graphic organizers on tests would be more creative, challenging, and fun than most traditional objective-style items.

Graphic organizers, therefore, are often used in the learning process during the formative stages of assessment. Teachers often use them to introduce topics, students use them to study, and sometimes students use them to present important information to other group members. What does not happen enough, however, is teachers using graphic organizers for assessments or evaluation.

Why not ask students to select a graphic organizer to take the place of an essay? Why couldn't students complete a right-angle thinking model listing the facts on the right and their feelings or associations about the topic on the bottom? Why not ask the students to fill in a Venn diagram comparing the works of Hemingway and Faulkner? Give them points for every correct characteristic they feel the authors have in common (middle area) and points for each of the characteristics they feel is different (outside circles). Including graphic organizers on tests would be more creative, challenging, and fun than most traditional objective-style items. Teachers could also require a paragraph or an oral presentation discussing the different elements of the graphic organizer as part of the test.

Ideas for using graphic organizers include the following:
1. Include graphic organizers on quizzes and tests.
2. Require groups to complete an assigned graphic organizer and topic on newsprint. Give group grade for final graphic organizer and oral presentation.
3. Assign students to select one graphic organizer to use to analyze a lecture, video, book, piece of fiction, piece of non-fiction, speech, news story, or textbook reading. Grade the assignment on accuracy, originality, and creativity.
4. Allow the students to select one or two graphic organizer assignments from their work to include in the portfolio.
5. Assign students work that requires a graphic organizer to be completed by a cooperative group. Ask each student in the group to complete an individual writing or speaking assignment based on the ideas included in the graphic organizer. Give a group grade and an individual grade.

6. Ask the students or the cooperative group to invent an original graphic organizer. Grade the assignment on the basis of originality, creativity, usefulness, and logic.

7. Require students to utilize a graphic organizer in a project or oral presentation. Grade the quality and effectiveness of the original organizer.

8. Create a picture graphic organizer that includes outlines of objects rather than circles or lines.

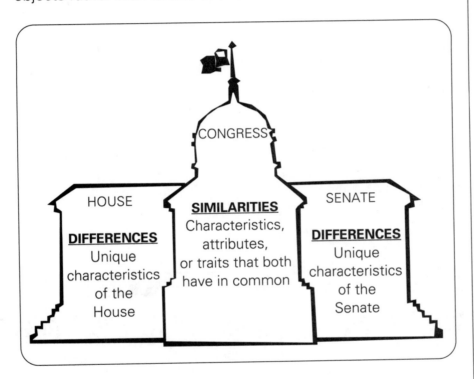

CONGRESS

HOUSE

DIFFERENCES
Unique characteristics of the House

SIMILARITIES
Characteristics, attributes, or traits that both have in common

SENATE

DIFFERENCES
Unique characteristics of the Senate

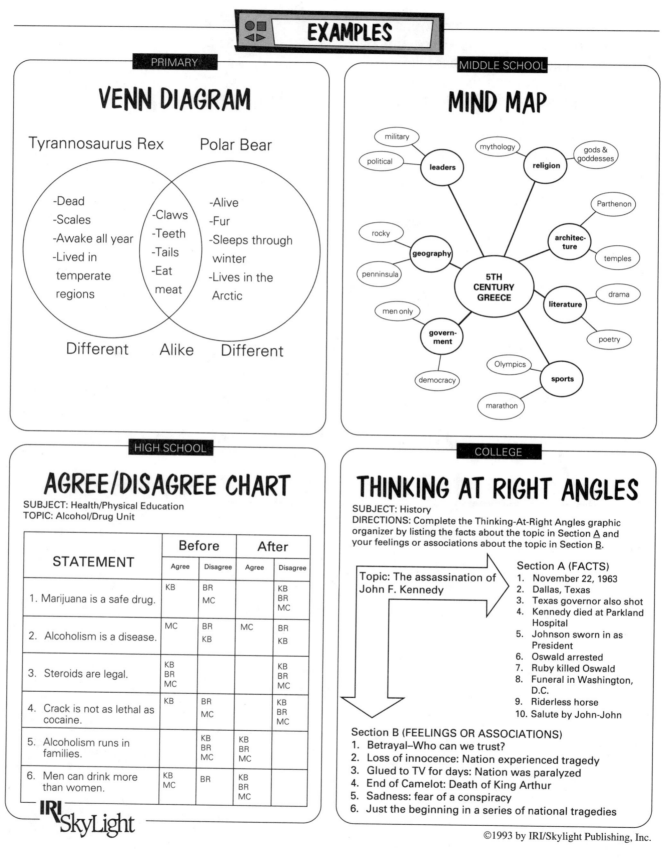

EXAMPLES

PRIMARY

VENN DIAGRAM

Tyrannosaurus Rex   Polar Bear

-Dead
-Scales
-Awake all year
-Lived in
 temperate
 regions

-Claws
-Teeth
-Tails
-Eat
 meat

-Alive
-Fur
-Sleeps through
 winter
-Lives in the
 Arctic

Different   Alike   Different

MIDDLE SCHOOL

MIND MAP

military
political
leaders
mythology
religion
gods &
goddesses
rocky
geography
penninsula
5TH
CENTURY
GREECE
architec-
ture
Parthenon
temples
literature
drama
poetry
men only
govern-
ment
democracy
Olympics
sports
marathon

HIGH SCHOOL

AGREE/DISAGREE CHART

SUBJECT: Health/Physical Education
TOPIC: Alcohol/Drug Unit

STATEMENT	Before		After	
	Agree	Disagree	Agree	Disagree
1. Marijuana is a safe drug.	KB	BR MC		KB BR MC
2. Alcoholism is a disease.	MC	BR KB	MC	BR KB
3. Steroids are legal.	KB BR MC			KB BR MC
4. Crack is not as lethal as cocaine.	KB	BR MC		KB BR MC
5. Alcoholism runs in families.		KB BR MC	KB BR MC	
6. Men can drink more than women.	KB MC	BR	KB BR MC	

COLLEGE

THINKING AT RIGHT ANGLES

SUBJECT: History
DIRECTIONS: Complete the Thinking-At-Right Angles graphic organizer by listing the facts about the topic in Section <u>A</u> and your feelings or associations about the topic in Section <u>B</u>.

Topic: The assassination of John F. Kennedy

Section A (FACTS)
1. November 22, 1963
2. Dallas, Texas
3. Texas governor also shot
4. Kennedy died at Parkland Hospital
5. Johnson sworn in as President
6. Oswald arrested
7. Ruby killed Oswald
8. Funeral in Washington, D.C.
9. Riderless horse
10. Salute by John-John

Section B (FEELINGS OR ASSOCIATIONS)
1. Betrayal–Who can we trust?
2. Loss of innocence: Nation experienced tragedy
3. Glued to TV for days: Nation was paralyzed
4. End of Camelot: Death of King Arthur
5. Sadness: fear of a conspiracy
6. Just the beginning in a series of national tragedies

IRI SkyLight

AGREE/DISAGREE STATEMENTS

Directions: Write statements about a topic your students will study. Give to groups of students *before* and *after* the unit.

TOPIC: _____

STATEMENT: _____	BEFORE		AFTER	
	Agree	Disagree	Agree	Disagree
1.				
2.				
3.				
4.				
5.				
6.				
7.				
8.				
9.				
10.				

IRISkyLight

THINKING AT RIGHT ANGLES

Directions: Select a topic and ask students to list the facts about it in column A and their feelings and associations in column B.

TOPIC: _____

FACTS

FEELINGS AND ASSOCIATIONS

A

_____
_____
_____
_____
_____
_____
_____
_____

B

_____
_____
_____
_____
_____

IRI SkyLight

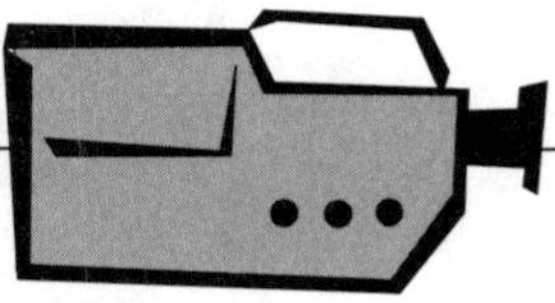

GRAPHIC ORGANIZERS
REFLECTION PAGE

RECORD

1. Think about how you can use graphic organizers in your lessons. Which organizers might work best with your students? Why?

_____

_____

_____

_____

_____

_____

_____

_____

_____

_____

_____

_____

_____

_____

2. Create a new idea for a graphic organizer or ask your students to create an original graphic organizer that contains pictures or graphics.

IRI *SkyLight*

Notes:

Use Venne diagroms for
compare + contrast

INTERVIEWS AND CONFERENCES

CHAPTER **11**

"Because of time constraints, students often have few opportunities to write or speak more than a sentence or two. This is unfortunate, since most people would probably agree that the best way to determine whether a person understands a subject or problem is simply to ask him or her to *explain* and to respond to questions that the explanation itself is likely to provoke."

-Archbald & Newmann, 1988, p. 13

WHAT ARE INTERVIEWS AND CONFERENCES?

Stiggins states that there are three categories of assessment methods available to gauge student attainment of teacher expectations:

1. Paper-and-pencil assessments
2. Performance assessments (or measures based on observation and judgment)
3. Direct personal communication with the student

He says that the third category, personal communication, can take the form of "student answers to questions during instruction, interviews and conversations with students, and intuitions and feelings about students" (Stiggins, 1991, p. 537). Each of these three methods yields legitimate achievement data if the teacher knows how to develop the "rules of evidence" correctly.

Teachers, however, are generally reluctant to utilize direct personal communication with the student as legitimate assessment because they feel it is too subjective. Imagine how shaky a teacher would feel telling a parent "I have an intuition or gut feeling that Bradley doesn't cooperate effectively." Yet, conferences and interviews can be structured to yield legitimate achievement data as well as monitor students' attitudes and feelings.

Types of Interviews and Conferences

Teachers can utilize both formal and informal interviews and conferences:

1. Interview about a book with one student or group of students
2. Discussion of a group or an individual project
3. Interview about a research paper or project
4. Reactions to a film or video
5. Feedback from a field trip
6. Reactions to assemblies or guest speakers
7. Discussion of a piece of writing
8. Interview in a foreign language to check for fluency and grammar

PAUSE

Teachers are generally reluctant to utilize direct personal communication with the student as legitimate assessment because they feel it is too subjective.

9. Feelings about works of art or music pieces
10. Discussion about problem solving
11. Interview about a scientific experiment
12. Attitudes about a course or the school
13. Conference about the portfolio
14. Discussion about dynamics of cooperative groups
15. Discussion of students' grades and future goals
16. Feelings about sportsmanship
17. Steps to fix a car
18. Questions about the process in a paper or project
19. Selection process for the portfolio
20. Discussion of quarterly grades

Student interviews and conferences reinforce the outcome of communication. Students should be encouraged to engage in oral interactions on a daily basis, and these authentic assessments provide that opportunity.

PAUSE

Sometimes talking to students is the most effective way to assess what many younger students know and feel.

WHY SHOULD WE USE INTERVIEWS AND CONFERENCES?

Primary teachers have probably based more assessment on "direct personal communication with the student" than teachers in the middle school or high school. Sometimes talking to students is the most effective way to assess what many younger students know and feel.

The Ministry of Education in British Columbia published a booklet in 1991 entitled *Supporting Learning: Understanding and Assessing the Progress of Children in the Primary Program*. In a section titled, "How We Find Out What a Child Can Do" the text reads: "Teachers collect information about a child's progress in the same way that parents collect information about their child's growth and learning. They watch children in action, look at collections of children's work and talk with children. In the Primary Program this is called 'collecting authentic evidence'" (p. 13).

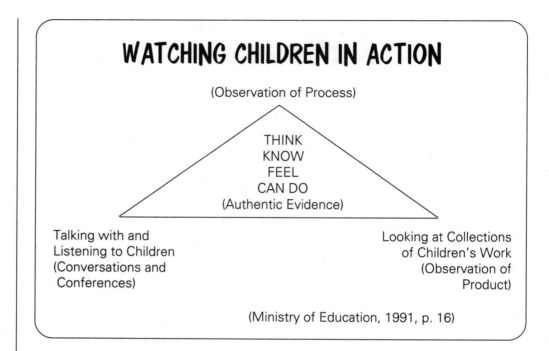

WATCHING CHILDREN IN ACTION

(Observation of Process)

THINK
KNOW
FEEL
CAN DO
(Authentic Evidence)

Talking with and
Listening to Children
(Conversations and
Conferences)

Looking at Collections
of Children's Work
(Observation of
Product)

(Ministry of Education, 1991, p. 16)

PAUSE

The interactions that take place in a learner-focused classroom enhance the communication skills of the students and provide valuable assessment tools for the teacher.

If teachers talk with and listen to students, they can gather information that sometimes cannot be gathered any other way. When talking with and listening to children in school, teachers can use the information to:

- help clarify thinking
- assist children to think about their own learning
- help achieve new levels of understanding
- facilitate self-evaluation
- make them feel their ideas and opinions are valued
- help children appreciate progress and set future goals
- respond to their comments
- build positive teacher-child relationships
- lead them to become self-directed learners
                            (Ministry of Education, 1991, p. 16)

In interviews, conferences, and conversations, students get the opportunity to refine and clarify their thinking and respond to others. Additionally, talking about what they have done and what they plan to do is essential if students are going to learn how to evaluate themselves. The interactions that take place in a learner-focused classroom enhance the communication skills of the students and provide valuable assessment tools for the teacher.

HOW SHOULD WE ASSESS INTERVIEWS AND CONFERENCES?

Some schools are now mandating that teachers conduct conferences with individual students at least once a month. But in order to do that, elementary teachers would have to conduct one conference a day, and secondary teachers may have to conduct as many as five a day. And what are the other students supposed to be doing when the teacher is conferencing with a student? Many teachers are experimenting with allowing other students to do group work or independent work while they are talking with one student. Some are also conducting group conferences or allowing students to do peer conferences with "guiding questions" to help the student focus on key points.

Kallick says that the "quality of the conference is far more significant than the quantity of conferences" (1992, p. 314). She asks teachers to imagine that they are able to resurrect someone like John Dewey or Jean Piaget for only fifteen minutes. Most of the questions would elicit responses that only Dewey or Piaget could provide. Questions like "What was on your mind when...?" or "Now that you have accomplished your work, what do you think about...?" would yield provocative answers. These types of questions could only be answered by a primary source—why then waste precious time by asking low-level questions like "Where were you born?" or "How did you die?"

Why not treat the few minutes with each student the same way? Why not ask higher-order questions that access the student's thoughts or feelings? Don't ask questions about grades or test results that are available from the gradebook.

Sample Questions for Student Interview
How did you feel about our unit on poetry?
How do you feel about your writing?
In your opinion, why is it important to keep a portfolio?

Interviews and conferences, therefore, should play an important role in the assessment process in all classrooms—from kindergarten to graduate school.

PAUSE

**"The quality of the conference is far more significant than the quantity of conferences."
-Kallick, 1992, p. 314**

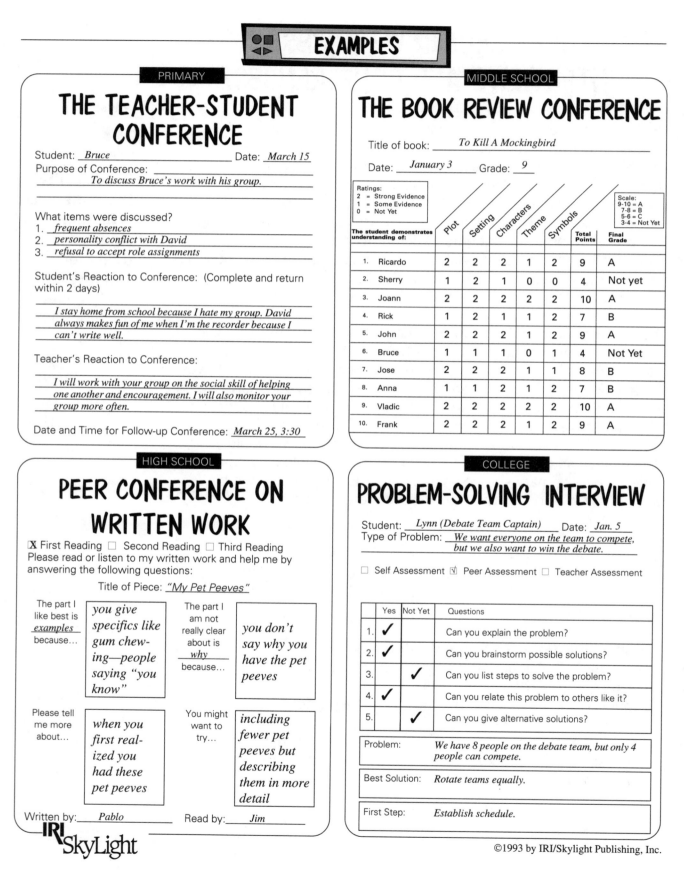

EXAMPLES

PRIMARY

THE TEACHER-STUDENT CONFERENCE

Student: _Bruce_   Date: _March 15_

Purpose of Conference: _____
_____ To discuss Bruce's work with his group. _____
_____

What items were discussed?
1. _frequent absences_
2. _personality conflict with David_
3. _refusal to accept role assignments_

Student's Reaction to Conference: (Complete and return within 2 days)

I stay home from school because I hate my group. David always makes fun of me when I'm the recorder because I can't write well.

Teacher's Reaction to Conference:

I will work with your group on the social skill of helping one another and encouragement. I will also monitor your group more often.

Date and Time for Follow-up Conference: _March 25, 3:30_

MIDDLE SCHOOL

THE BOOK REVIEW CONFERENCE

Title of book: _____ To Kill A Mockingbird _____

Date: _January 3_   Grade: _9_

Ratings:
2 = Strong Evidence
1 = Some Evidence
0 = Not Yet

Scale:
9-10 = A
7-8 = B
5-6 = C
3-4 = Not Yet

The student demonstrates understanding of:	Plot	Setting	Characters	Theme	Symbols	Total Points	Final Grade
1. Ricardo	2	2	2	1	2	9	A
2. Sherry	1	2	1	0	0	4	Not yet
3. Joann	2	2	2	2	2	10	A
4. Rick	1	2	1	1	2	7	B
5. John	2	2	2	1	2	9	A
6. Bruce	1	1	1	0	1	4	Not Yet
7. Jose	2	2	2	1	1	8	B
8. Anna	1	2	1	2	2	7	B
9. Vladic	2	2	2	2	2	10	A
10. Frank	2	2	2	1	2	9	A

HIGH SCHOOL

PEER CONFERENCE ON WRITTEN WORK

[X] First Reading ☐ Second Reading ☐ Third Reading
Please read or listen to my written work and help me by answering the following questions:

Title of Piece: _"My Pet Peeves"_

The part I like best is _examples_ because…	_you give specifics like gum chewing—people saying "you know"_	The part I am not really clear about is _why_ because…	_you don't say why you have the pet peeves_
Please tell me more about…	_when you first realized you had these pet peeves_	You might want to try…	_including fewer pet peeves but describing them in more detail_

Written by: _Pablo_   Read by: _Jim_

COLLEGE

PROBLEM-SOLVING INTERVIEW

Student: _Lynn (Debate Team Captain)_   Date: _Jan. 5_

Type of Problem: _We want everyone on the team to compete, but we also want to win the debate._

☐ Self Assessment   ☑ Peer Assessment   ☐ Teacher Assessment

	Yes	Not Yet	Questions
1.	✔		Can you explain the problem?
2.	✔		Can you brainstorm possible solutions?
3.		✔	Can you list steps to solve the problem?
4.	✔		Can you relate this problem to others like it?
5.		✔	Can you give alternative solutions?

Problem:	_We have 8 people on the debate team, but only 4 people can compete._
Best Solution:	_Rotate teams equally._
First Step:	_Establish schedule._

IRI SkyLight

ON YOUR OWN

PLAN A CONFERENCE

Directions: Have students create a list of questions they would want their teacher or their parents to ask them during a portfolio conference. Encourage the students to write higher-order questions that elicit reflective responses. (See Three-Story Intellect, p. 38)

QUESTIONS FOR MY PORTFOLIO CONFERENCE

1. _____

2. _____

3. _____

4. _____

5. _____

6. _____

IRISkyLight

INTERVIEW OR CONFERENCE

Develop an application of an interview or conference for your teaching.

BONUS

PEER CONFERENCE ON WRITTEN WORK

Directions: Have students exchange their written work with a partner and critique the work.

☐ First Reading   ☐ Second Reading   ☐ Third Reading

Please read or listen to my written work and help me by answering the following questions:

Title of Piece: _____

The part I like best is _____ because…

The part I am not really clear about is _____ because…

Please tell me more about…

You might want to try…

Written by:_____   Read by:_____

IRI SkyLight

INTERVIEW ON STUDENT PROJECTS

Student:_____ Date:_____

Subject Area: _____

1. What are you planning to do? _____
   _____
   _____

2. Tell me why you decided to do your project on the topic you chose?
   _____
   _____
   _____

3. Why do you think the project you selected is important?_____
   _____
   _____

4. Is anyone else going to help you? _____
   _____
   _____

5. Can you speculate how this project is relevant to life? _____
   _____
   _____

6. What skills or knowledge from other subject areas will you need to use to complete this project? _____
   _____
   _____

7. Do you need my help? _____
   _____
   _____

Teacher's signature: _____

IRI SkyLight

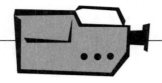

INTERVIEWS AND CONFERENCES
REFLECTION PAGE

RECORD

1. Reflect on the value of utilizing oral communication to find out what students know and how they feel.

_____

_____

_____

_____

_____

_____

_____

_____

_____

_____

2. Think of ways to assess interviews and conferences and how they can be included in the portfolio.

_____

_____

_____

_____

_____

_____

_____

_____

IRI SkyLight

Notes:

_____
_____
_____
_____
_____
_____
_____
_____
_____
_____
_____
_____
_____
_____
_____
_____
_____
_____
_____
_____
_____
_____
_____
_____
_____
_____
_____

THE FINAL GRADE

"Because the grading curve brands winners and losers, it works against the goal of successful learning for all students.... For every student who 'wins' with an A, there is one who 'loses' with a B, C, or F... Top scorers are motivated by their great grades to do better; poor grades in a competitive system only encourage the bottom scorers to languish or leave."

-James A. Bellanca, 1992b, p. 299

WHAT ARE FINAL GRADES?

"No level of education is free from it; no teacher or student can hide from it. The cry of 'Wad-Ja-Get?' is all around us…. Students, from kindergarten through graduate school, feel the ache of the 'Wad-Ja-Get?' syndrome; most know that it dominates more of their learning than they would ever care to admit" (Simon & Bellanca, 1976, p. 1). This quotation characterizes the type of competitive, bottom-line, win-at-any-cost mentality that is prevalent in schools and society. Students learn at an early age that they should get good grades if they want to impress and please their teachers and their parents. All A's on the report card is more important to most students than their love of learning. Students also know that they do not want to embarrass themselves by getting low grades, except of course, for those students who turn off to school early, and pride themselves on their "bad grades." Peer groups are often formed on the basis of grade point averages. The honor roll students usually do not mix well with the remedial borderline D/F students. A type of caste system usually forms in most schools by the middle school years based on report cards and tracking.

As much as most teachers hate to pass final judgment on a student by assigning one letter grade to summarize what a student can do, the reality is that most school systems still demand an account of how a student measures up.

The grading issue is very complex; moreover, it is also steeped in tradition. Teachers have been forced to become "bean counters" by adding up all the grades, bonus points, and minus points before using the calculator to divide by the total number of entries—to the second decimal point, of course. It's always amazing to see how much a student's final grade is lowered when one adds in all those minus points and zeros for missing homework assignments, forgetting to bring books, writing with pencil instead of pen, and the ultimate—tearing paper out of a spiral notebook instead of using loose-leaf! Sound ludicrous? Ask teachers and students if they have ever experienced or heard about these types of situations. Many people have experienced losing points or receiving Fs for writing on the back of the paper or forgetting to put their names on assignments. To say that the grading system in most American schools is archaic, inconsistent, and whimsical is an understatement. The final or summative

PAUSE

Students learn at an early age that they should get good grades if they want to impress and please their teachers and their parents.

grades in any course are probably the most difficult to assign because despite a student's rate of learning, ability level, special needs, or learning styles, he or she still has to be judged.

The Emphasis on Grades
The final grade in a class or year carries tremendous weight. The grade could determine promotion or retention in grade levels, participation in extracurricular activities, induction into a honor society, earning a college scholarship, or even graduating from high school. Yet, it is difficult to sum up all the multiple levels of learning and all the objectives or outcomes covered in a course with *one* letter or number grade.

Some educators advocate giving several final grades. For example, a report card might contain three grades—one grade to represent how a student has improved individually, the second to show how he or she compares to other students in the same grade level, and the third to represent how the student is doing compared to standards set by the district, state, or nation based on benchmarks or "exemplar" performances.

Many districts have eliminated traditional letter grades at the primary level and some others have eliminated them through eighth grade. The new report cards narrate how students have achieved thoughtful outcomes, as well as set new goals for students to grow without damaging their self-esteem. Across the country, the traditional report card is being replaced by assessment of portfolios, student-led conferences, anecdotal reports, narrative summaries, continuum of progress reports, student self-assessments, observation checklists, and other performance-based and more qualitative ways to assess student growth and development.

PAUSE

The new report cards narrate how students have achieved thoughtful outcomes, as well as set new goals for students to grow without damaging their self-esteem.

WHY DO WE NEED TO CHANGE OUR GRADING SYSTEM?

"Any information will have an effect upon the behavior of an individual only to the degree that he or she has discovered the personal meaning of that information for himself or herself.... This principle has vast implications for all aspects of education. It means that learning happens inside people; it is a subjective experience" (Combs, 1976, p. 6). Even though Combs quotation was written over twenty years ago, he addresses the same issue that Dewey and the constructivists address. Learning is *subjective*.

Importance of Self-Concept

The personal discovery of meaning by a student includes his or her feelings, attitudes, values, beliefs, hopes, and desires. This subjective experience, however, has to be objectified—broken down into discrete objectives and skills before it is meshed into one final grade. In this process, the self-concept of the student often suffers. Combs (1976) says that the new concept of learning emphasizes the crucial character of a student's self-concept.

"We now understand that an individual's self-concept determines his or her behavior in almost everything that person does. It also affects intelligence, for people who believe they are *able* will try, while those who believe they are *unable* will not" (Combs, 1976, p. 7).

Combs also states that people derive their self-concept from the *feedback* they receive from the people who surround them while they are growing up. Teachers provide much of that feedback via written and oral communication and, of course, grades. Poor grades, especially as early as kindergarten and first grade, can have a negative impact on a student. Moreover, classification in a "lower track" exacerbates the student's poor self-concept because now not only the teacher and student recognize the problem but everybody—counselors, parents, students, teachers, and administrators—know the student has a "problem." How many students have been negatively influenced by "feedback" from teachers? And most importantly, how many times has this negative feedback in the form of comments and grades become a self-fulfilling prophecy for the student?

Competition

In addition to the inequities in the grading system and the damage traditional grades do to the self-concept of many students, the emphasis on competition to achieve higher grades or higher groups also weakens the learning process. Competition for grades, reading groups, honor rolls, and scholarships probably *weakens* the educational system because it separates the "winners" from the "losers." First graders learn early on that the "Robin" reading groups are the winners and the "Buzzards" are the losers.

Kohn (1992) attacks the sacred cow of competition by stating that competition is not part of human nature. Instead, it poisons relationships, hurts self-esteem, and impedes excellence. If students are constantly competing for the highest grade in the class, the honor roll, or for class valedictorian, they often lose sight of one of the most

PAUSE

People derive their self-concept from the *feedback* they receive from the people who surround them while they are growing up.

142

thoughtful outcomes of all—collaboration. How can students be taught to cooperate with group members, share, teach each other, and compromise when their major concern is to beat out everyone else, get ahead, come out on top, and, at all costs, win!

Contrary to a long-held American tradition, individuals who work alone, compete against everyone around them, and value winning above all else do not necessarily come out on top, nor do they necessarily make good students or employees. Report after report from business leaders and from the SCANS Report issued by the U.S. Department of Labor (1992) stress the importance of cooperation in the workplace. People who can listen to others, work together, share ideas, and cooperate often contribute more to the overall effectiveness of a company than most individualistic, competitive people. Therefore, educators and parents who emphasize competition, high grades at any cost, and the ultimate weapon—the grading curve— may be doing a disservice to students. A major paradigm shift needs to occur so that society values cooperation, responsibility, and altruism and so that these values are modeled and taught in the schools.

Cheating by Students

Another reason the current grading system must be re-evaluated and reformed is the fact that it leads to cheating—an inevitable by-product of the grading system. Cheating in American schools is epidemic. Many students from kindergarten through college engage in cheating to pass a course or get a higher grade. Cheating can involve plagiarizing term papers or book reports, copying another's test answers, talking to other students who took the test, stealing tests or teacher's edition of books, or altering grades in a grade book. It is all the result of too much pressure being placed on students to "make the grade."

Students will often cheat:
1. to avoid failing a test
2. to avoid being branded "stupid" by peers
3. to avoid punishment by parents (losing privileges)
4. to try out for the team or cheerleading squad
5. to participate in extracurricular activites
6. to get on the honor roll
7. to avoid being sent to remedial classes
8. to get accepted to college
9. to win a scholarship to college
10. for the thrill of it

PAUSE

Another reason the current grading system must be re-evaluated and reformed is the fact that it leads to cheating—an inevitable by-product of the grading system.

The current grading system exerts enormous pressure on many students to compete and sometimes to cheat in order to succeed. Posting grades on the blackboard, publishing honor rolls, awarding bonus points, candy, free recess, or field trips for high scores, assigning students to "gifted classes" on the basis of test scores, and honoring students who receive the highest grades at all-school assemblies all promote a heavy emphasis on the grading process.

Education can be reduced to a quantifiable objective process rather than a qualitative affective process. At a very early age, students learn to cope with the system, and by the time they get to high school, Glasser says as many as fifty percent of secondary students have become what he calls "unsatisfied students." The "unsatisfied" student makes no consistent effort to learn. "All living creatures, and we are no exception, only do what they believe is most satisfying to them, and the main reason our schools are less effective than we would like them to be is that, where students are concerned, we have failed to appreciate this fact." (Glasser, 1986, p. 8)

By the time a student gets to high school, he or she may have faced hundreds of humiliations because of low grades. It is no wonder self-concept suffers and many students choose to "act out," "drop out," or "cheat" to escape the endless pressure to pass. In addition, the frustration of trying hard but still receiving poor grades because of learning or behavior disabilities discourages and frustrates many students. The need of the system to collect, analyze, and compare grades overrides the need of the student to construct knowledge for himself, to feel good about himself, and to enjoy learning.

Cheating by Educators

Cheating, unfortunately, is not limited to students. Cheating moves beyond the classroom right into competition between schools and districts to get the top scores. Realtors often quote the rankings of neighborhood schools when they are trying to sell homes. Standardized test scores are published in the paper and principals' and superintendents' reputations and jobs are sometimes built on test scores. More and more cheating scandals about teachers coaching students

PAUSE

The need of the system to collect, analyze, and compare grades overrides the need of the student to construct knowledge for himself, to feel good about himself, and to enjoy learning.

for tests or principals prompting and preparing teachers and students are appearing as the battle to be number one continues. An unhealthy emphasis on competition, standardized test scores, and grades often starts at the top of the educational system and then filters down to the teachers and students.

HOW CAN WE CHANGE THE GRADING SYSTEM?

Even if educators agree that the present grading system has become a hydra-headed monster that has overshadowed, intimidated, and, in some cases, debilitated students, the fact remains that in most cases the elimination of traditional letter and number grades on report cards is not yet a reality. For most teachers, district mandates, college requirements, and parental pressures dictate that grades in some form are a "nonnegotiable" requirement. If districts are required to give grades, are there ways to give more authentic grades that measure growth, development, and performance on the thoughtful outcomes established at the beginning of the year? Are there ways to give grades to help students to grow rather than to help them compete in the "Wad-Ja-Get?" syndrome?

How to Grade, If You Must

Grading Options
The following grading options can be used alone or in combination with other options to arrive at a final evaluation.

1. **Anecdotal Report Card**
   The Ministry of Education in British Columbia, Canada requires a Primary Progress Report that provides a narrative report on the front and a list of the Primary Program Goals and criteria on the back.

PAUSE

Are there ways to give grades to help students to grow rather than to help them compete in the "Wad-Ja-Get?" syndrome?

Anecdotal Report Card

MINISTRY OF EDUCATION: PRIMARY PROGRESS REPORT

Student's Name:_____

School: _____ District:_____

Reporting Period:_____ Date: _____

The goals of the Primary Program are to provide a variety of experiences that foster the child.

- Aesthetic and Artistic Development
- Physical Development
- Emotional and Social Development
- Social Responsibility
- Intellectual Development

All goals are emphasized throughout the entire program.

❑ Continuing in the Primary Program
❑ Beginning the Intermediate Program

Parents: Please keep this copy and return the report card cover only. Thank you.

2. The Traditional Grade

Each assignment is graded according to specific predetermined criteria. Once all the grades from assignments, projects, performances, and tests are entered into the gradebook, the teacher adds all the scores and divides by the total number of scores to determine the final grade.

The Traditional Grade

COURSE: AMERICAN LITERATURE

Tests, Assignments, Projects	Grade
1. Test on Puritan Unit	94
2. Learning Logs	90
3. Reflective Journals	93
4. Observation Checklist on Social Skills	85
5. Exhibition of Salem Witch Trial	96
6. Colonial Newspaper Project	91
7. Group Project on Hawthorne	88
8. Test on *The Scarlet Letter*	83
9. Portfolio	<u>90</u>
	810 points

810 points divided by 9 = 90
Final Grade = 90 (B+)

---

3. Assessment of Thoughtful Outcomes

Essential outcomes can be assessed by asking both the student and the teacher to list evidence of achieving the outcomes. The teacher reads the students' self-assessment, writes his or her own evaluation, and then determines the final grade.

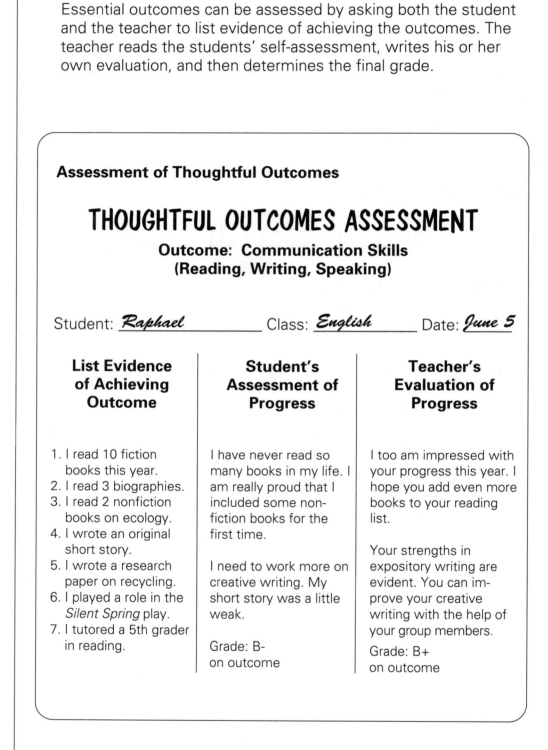

Assessment of Thoughtful Outcomes

THOUGHTFUL OUTCOMES ASSESSMENT

Outcome: Communication Skills
(Reading, Writing, Speaking)

Student: *Raphael*   Class: *English*   Date: *June 5*

List Evidence of Achieving Outcome	Student's Assessment of Progress	Teacher's Evaluation of Progress
1. I read 10 fiction books this year. 2. I read 3 biographies. 3. I read 2 nonfiction books on ecology. 4. I wrote an original short story. 5. I wrote a research paper on recycling. 6. I played a role in the *Silent Spring* play. 7. I tutored a 5th grader in reading.	I have never read so many books in my life. I am really proud that I included some non-fiction books for the first time. I need to work more on creative writing. My short story was a little weak. Grade: B- on outcome	I too am impressed with your progress this year. I hope you add even more books to your reading list. Your strengths in expository writing are evident. You can improve your creative writing with the help of your group members. Grade: B+ on outcome

Mrs. Jones and Tommy both reflect on their thoughtful outcomes for the new school year.

PAUSE

The purpose of the portfolios is to show growth and development over time and to allow interactive dialogue about a student's strengths, weaknesses, and future goals.

4. Non-Graded Portfolio

The portfolio provides one of the richest opportunities for a final course evaluation. Chapter four of this book reviews many of the options teachers can exercise with portfolios. One option is to grade work as students complete it throughout the grading period. The work is graded on the basis of predetermined criteria, returned to the students with feedback, and stored in a folder or file.

At the end of the grading period, students select key items to display in the portfolio. They often reflect on why they included the pieces, and they share their portfolios with peers, teachers, and parents during portfolio conferences. The purpose of the portfolios is to show growth and development over time and to allow interactive dialogue about a student's strengths, weaknesses, and future goals. The portfolio is not graded; it serves instead as a compilation of pieces that represent the student's work and the student's progress.

5. The Final Graded Portfolio

Some educators, especially at the high school level, find they can motivate students more when the final portfolio is graded. They give regular grades throughout the class for quizzes, tests, homework, and other assignments. However, the portfolio at the end of the course is given a final grade that is usually weighted more (20-50% of the total grade). Students, therefore, might not do well on traditional quizzes and tests, but they have a chance to work hard and still succeed by doing a good job on the portfolio.

For example, students keep most of their work in a file folder in the classroom. This file folder is called the "Working Portfolio." Throughout the course, the teacher tells the students to select something from their "Working Portfolio" to go into their "Final Portfolio." Often the teacher tells the student what to select, but other times the students have some choice.

PAUSE

Teachers who have incorporated some type of portfolio assessment into their curriculum are excited about the quality of work the students produce.

Students then have a chance to revise things and make them better. The students also know up front what the criteria are for each assignment so they know the standards by which the teacher will grade them. Instead of grading all the logs, journals, and assignments students complete, teachers will have to grade only the portfolio contents. They will also be able to grade them more fairly and consistently because of the predetermined criteria, and they will have more time to provide constructive feedback.

Each teacher needs to explore how he or she can utilize the portfolio system as a method of evaluation. Teachers who have incorporated some type of portfolio assessment into their curriculum are excited about the quality of work the students produce, their motivation to learn, and their pride of accomplishment. The finished product of a portfolio and the interaction of a portfolio conference provide a richness, a sense of accomplishment, and a sense of understanding rarely derived from a single number or letter grade on a report card.

Final Graded Portfolio

FINAL PORTFOLIO

Student: *Carol B.*   Class: *Geometry*   Date: *May 26*

Selections	Grade	Comments
1. Geometric drawings	95	You have done a beautiful job drawing and labeling the angles.
2. Research report on "Why Math"	92	The research you did on the relevancy of math to our lives helped you see its importance.
3. Learning logs	90	I can see how you were having problems understanding the new concepts.
4. Reflective journals	94	Your frustration on tests is evident from your journal. You seem to be working through your anxiety.
5. Problem-solving logs	75	You still need to explore alternative solutions when you can't solve a problem.
6. Profile of math-related professions	91	You made the transfer of math from the classroom to the outside world.
7. Student self-evaluation for course*	89	I gave myself an 89 because I like math, but I still can't solve problems on my own.
Total Points 626 ÷ 7 = 89.4	Final Grade 89	It's interesting that your average is the same as your own self-evaluation!

*Self-evaluation grade is provided by the student

Comments: Your writing and research skills and appreciation of why math is important are excellent. Even though you feel math is your weakest subject, you are making great strides to overcome your phobia and solve problems.

Suggested Future Goals: Work with your cooperative group more. Ask them to "talk out loud" when they are solving problems so you can see their thought processes.

Final portfolio grade =   89 (50%)

Average grade for other work = 83 (50%)

Final grade for class = 86 (B) Teacher: *Lois Meyers*

EXAMPLES

PRIMARY

PROGRESS REPORT

Grade: <u>First</u>

Student: <u>Juan Carlos</u>

Marking
Period: <u>Weeks 1-12</u>

	First 6 Weeks			Second 6 Weeks		
	Not Yet	With Support	Independently	Not Yet	With Support	Independently
SPEAKING BEHAVIOR						
Communicates appropriately	✓					✓
Speaks in logical sequence		✓				✓
Participates	✓			✓		
LISTENING BEHAVIOR						
Listens to speaker	✓			✓		
Responds appropriately		✓				✓
Asks key questions	✓					✓

COMMENTS: Juan has developed good speaking skills, but he still needs to work on listening to his group members.

MIDDLE SCHOOL

PROGRESS REPORT

Student: <u>Eric Smith</u>   Grade: <u>8th</u>

ATTENDANCE	QUARTER			
	1	2	3	4
DAYS PRESENT	60	55	50	52
DAYS ABSENT	0	5	10	8
DAYS TARDY 0	3	5	3	

GRADING SCALE
M = Most of the Time
S = Sometimes
N = Not Yet

	QUARTER			
	1	2	3	4
ENGLISH				
• Makes Predictions	S	S	S	S
• Demonstrates Active Interest	M	S	S	S
• Able to Speak in Front of Groups	M	M	M	M
• Listens to and Follows Directions	S	M	S	M
PHYSICAL EDUCATION				
• Performs Skills Well	N	S	S	M
• Positive Attitude and Effort	N	N	S	S
MATHEMATICS				
• Demonstrates a Concept of No.s	M	M	M	M
• Demonstrates Computational Skills	N	S	S	S
• Demonstrates Measurement Skills	S	S	S	S
ART				
• Performs Skills Well	M	M	M	M
• Positive Attitude and Effort	M	M	M	M

HIGH SCHOOL

REPORT CARD

Student: <u>Betrina Gregory</u>   Semester: <u>1st</u>
Grade: <u>10th</u>

Class: <u>English</u>
Speaking   Final Grade: <u>B-</u>
—/————/————X—/—
NOT YET   C   A

Writing
—/————/————X/—
NOT YET   C   A

Reading
Comprehension
—/————/——X—/—
NOT YET   C   A

Class: <u>Mathematics</u>   Final Grade: <u>A-</u>
Reasoning
—/————/————/X
NOT YET   C   A

Problem Solving
—/————/————/— X
NOT YET   C   A

Computational Skills
—/————/——X——/—
NOT YET   C   A

Class: <u>Social Studies</u>   Final Grade: <u>C</u>
Cooperation
—/——X——/————/—
NOT YET   C   A

Research Skills
—/————X——/————/—
NOT YET   C   A

Analysis
—/——X————/————/—
NOT YET   C   A

COLLEGE

REPORT CARD

Student: <u>Michael Brown</u>   Semester: <u>2nd</u>

ECONOMICS   Grade: <u>B</u>
Strengths: <u>Budget planning, inflation</u>

Areas to Develop: <u>Understanding of different economic systems</u>

Teacher: Ruth Jones

BIOLOGY   Grade: <u>C</u>
Strengths: <u>Classification, analysis, problem solving</u>

Areas to Develop: <u>Writing effective lab reports</u>
Teacher: Chris Roberts

CIVICS: Grade: <u>A</u>
Strengths: <u>Government agencies, state and local governments</u>

Areas to Develop: <u>The U.S. election process at the national level</u>

Teacher: Bob Adams

IRI SkyLight

FINAL GRADE PLAN

Select a grade or course you teach. Plan how you will evaluate the entire course. Prepare a one-page evaluation sheet showing the students what is required and how the whole package will be graded in order to arrive at a final grade.

REPORT CARD REVISION

Revise the report card or grading document you currently use to reflect a more meaningful evaluation process.

IRI/SkyLight

RECORD

THE FINAL GRADE
REFLECTION PAGE

1. How did you feel about grades when you were in school? Did you ever receive a grade that you felt was unfair? Explain.

    _____

    _____

    _____

    _____

    _____

    _____

    _____

    _____

    _____

    _____

2. Reflect on your feelings about the grading process currently in place in your school. Could you offer suggestions to improve the process?

    _____

    _____

    _____

    _____

    _____

    _____

    _____

Notes:

_____

_____

_____

_____

_____

_____

_____

_____

_____

_____

_____

_____

_____

_____

_____

_____

_____

_____

_____

_____

_____

_____

_____

_____

_____

CONCLUSION

"As at the last judgment, students are sorted into the wheat and the chaff. Rewards of *A's* and *B's* go out to the good, and punishments of *F's* are doled out to the bad. 'Gifts' of *D's* (*D's* are always gifts) are meted out, and *C's* (that wonderfully tepid grade) are bestowed on those whose names teachers can rarely remember."
-Majesky, 1993, p. 88

This quotation from the introduction of the book summarizes why the traditional method of assigning one letter or number grade to sum up a student's performance over a semester or year has to change. Assigning final grades can be a gut-wrenching task. Most first grade teachers agonize over giving letter grades to their students. How ridiculous to classify students at such an early age, regardless of their readiness level, socioeconomic background, or social or academic development. Most first graders do not even understand the concept of a grade other than "Mommy and Daddy are happy when I bring home an 'A'."

Despite all the publicity about standardized tests, it is really the solitary teacher who ultimately passes judgments on students by filling in the final grade on the report card—a grade that determines placement in specific classes, participation in extracurricular activities, promotion or retention, class ranking, school honor roll, National Honor Society, class valedictorian, career opportunities, college admissions, or college scholarships. Moreover, these grades are not always based on clear and specific criteria or standards. Sometimes they are influenced by student behavior, are subjective, and are based on busywork or low-level quizzes and tests. It is no wonder the traditional grading system in schools is being questioned.

"Teachers no longer command the automatic respect of their charges, no longer wield great paddles to enforce discipline, no longer are considered the last bastion of knowledge. But the giving of the grade makes up for some of that. It marks the lives of those who receive it. It may not be imprinted on the forehead, but it certainly leaves an impression" (Majesky, 1993, p. 88).

PAUSE

It is really the solitary teacher who ultimately passes judgments on students by filling in the final grade on the report card.

PAUSE

Assigning grades on the basis of multiple-choice tests, pop quizzes, lower-level thinking, homework, and drill-and-skill worksheets will soon be as obsolete as the old mimeograph machine.

Like the scarlet letter of Puritan times, the mark the grade leaves on each student can affect the psyche, self-esteem, and self-confidence of a student. It can also label, track, and rank the student. The grade can also be a formidable instrument if used to discipline and control students and to coerce them into "staying within the lines." Teachers and district administrators need to re-examine grading procedures by talking with other districts that have eliminated traditional grades in elementary schools and replaced them with anecdotal report cards and conferences that address specific learner outcomes rather than compress a plethora of skills, experiences, and feelings into *one* grade.

The assessment ideas presented in this book are merely the tip of the iceberg. Individual teachers and teams of teachers can work with students to construct original assessment strategies to measure student growth. Politicians, publishers, and parents need to be informed that the real core curriculum is *not* the content but is instead the thoughtful outcomes such as critical and creative thinking, collaboration, decision making, and problem solving. Multiple-choice Scantron tests alone cannot measure the meaningful outcomes that are worth teaching. Assigning grades on the basis of multiple-choice tests, pop quizzes, lower-level thinking, homework, and drill-and-skill worksheets will soon be as obsolete as the old mimeograph machine.

The standardized test score, grades on quizzes and tests, and final report card grade are just a few isolated, flat, and one-dimensional pictures of a student. Those pictures may have been adequate in the Polaroid and Instamatic schools of yesterday, but they are too superficial for the restructured school of today. No teacher, parent, or student in the high-tech age of the 21st century will settle for a few snapshots to summarize a student's academic life when camcorders can capture every nuance of a child's development. The "videotape" is an effective metaphor for authentic assessment because both can paint a rich and multidimensional portrait of "a student in motion," a student engaged in a wide variety of authentic tasks, and a student who is in control of his or her own educational process.

In the mindful school, students become the technical engineers of their own academic videos. They can review what they have accomplished, stop the tape, rewind and do something over, fast forward over things they already know, and, of course, edit as needed. When students monitor their own learning, they internalize the process of evaluation. And after all, the internalization of self-evaluation is one of the most important skills of all. "We must constantly remind our-selves that the ultimate purpose of evaluation is to have students become self-evaluating. If students graduate from our schools still dependent upon others to tell them when they are adequate, good, or excellent, then we've missed the whole point of what education is about" (Costa & Kallick, 1992, p. 280).

BIBLIOGRAPHY

Archbald, D. A., & Newmann, F. M. (1988). *Beyond standardized testing: Assessing authentic academic achievement in the secondary school.* Madison: University of Wisconsin, National Association of Secondary School Principals.

Barell, J. (1992). Like an incredibly hard algebra problem: Teaching for metacognition. In A. L. Costa, J. A. Bellanca, & R. Fogarty (Eds.), *If minds matter: A foreword to the future, Volume I* (pp. 257–266). Palatine, IL: IRI/Skylight Publishing, Inc.

Bednar, A. K., Cunningham, D., Duffy, T. M., & Perry, J. D. (1993). Theory into practice: How do we link? In G. Anglin (Ed.), *Instructional technology: Past, present, and future.* Denver, CO: Libraries Unlimited.

Bellanca, J. A. (1992). Classroom 2001: Evolution, not revolution. In A. L. Costa, J. A. Bellanca, & R. Fogarty (Eds.), *If minds matter: A foreword to the future, Volume II* (pp. 161–165). Palatine, IL: IRI/Skylight Publishing, Inc.

Bellanca, J. A. (1992a). *The cooperative think tank II: Graphic organizers to teach thinking in the cooperative classroom.* Palatine, IL: IRI/Skylight Publishing, Inc.

Bellanca, J. A. (1992b). How to grade (if you must). In A. L. Costa, J. A. Bellanca, & R. Fogarty (Eds.), *If minds matter: A foreword to the future, Volume II* (pp. 297–311). Palatine, IL: IRI/Skylight Publishing, Inc.

Bellanca, J. A., & Fogarty, R. (1991). *Blueprints for thinking in the cooperative classroom* (2nd ed.). Palatine, IL: IRI/Skylight Publishing, Inc.

Black, H., & Black, S. (1990). *Organizing thinking: Graphic organizers, Book II.* Pacific Grove, CA: Midwest Publications Critical Thinking Press and Software.

Board of Education for the City of Etobicoke. (1987). *Making the grade: Evaluating student progress.* Scarborough, Ontario, Canada: Prentice-Hall Canada.

Brandt, R. (1992a, May). On performance assessment: A conversation with Grant Wiggins. *Educational Leadership,* pp. 35–37.

Brandt, R. (1992b, May). Overview: A fresh focus for curriculum. *Educational Leadership,* p. 7.

Brown, R. (1989, April). Testing and thoughtfulness. *Educational Leadership,* pp. 113–115.

Brownlie, F., Close, S., & Wingren, L. (1990). *Tomorrow's classroom today.* Portsmouth, NH: Heinemann.

Brownlie, F., Close, S., & Wingren, L. (1988). *Reaching for higher thought: Reading, writing, thinking strategies.* Edmonton, Alberta, Canada: Arnold Publishing.

Burke, K. A. (Ed.). (1992a). *Authentic assessment: A collection.* Palatine, IL: IRI/Skylight Publishing, Inc.

Burke, K. A. (1992b). *What to do with the kid who...: Developing cooperation, self-discipline, and responsibility in the classroom.* Palatine, IL: IRI/Skylight Publishing, Inc.

Campbell, J. (1992, May). Laser disk portfolios: Total child assessment. *Educational Leadership,* pp. 69–70.

Chapman, C. (1993). *If the shoe fits. . .: How to use multiple intelligences in the classroom.* Palatine, IL: IRI/Skylight Publishing, Inc.

Cohen, M. (1980). *First grade takes a test.* New York: Dell Young Yearling, Bantam Doubleday Dell Publishing Group.

Combs, A. W. (1976). *What we know about learning and criteria for practice.* Adapted from a speech at the First National Conference on Grading Alternatives, Cleveland, OH. In Simon, S. B. & Bellanca, J. A. *Degrading the grading myths: A primer of alternatives to grades and marks,* (pp. 6–9). Washington, D.C.: Association for Supervision and Curriculum Development.

Congress of the United States, Office of Technology Assessment. (1992, March). *Testing in American schools: Asking the right questions.* Washington, D.C.: U.S. Government Printing Office.

Conner, K., Hairston, J., Hill, I., Kopple, H., Marshall, J., Scholnick, K., & Schulman, M. (1985, October). Using formative testing at the classroom, school and district levels. *Educational Leadership,* pp. 63–67.

Costa, A. L. (1991). *The school as a home for the mind: A collection of articles.* Palatine, IL: IRI/Skylight Publishing, Inc.

Costa, A. L., Bellanca, J. A., & Fogarty, R. (Eds.). (1992). *If minds matter: A foreword to the future, Volume I.* Palatine, IL: IRI/Skylight Publishing, Inc.

Costa, A. L., Bellanca, J. A., & Fogarty, R. (Eds.). (1992). *If minds matter: A foreword to the future, Volume II.* Palatine, IL: IRI/Skylight Publishing, Inc.

Costa, A. L., & Kallick, B. (1992). Reassessing assessment. In A.L. Costa, J. A. Bellanca, & R. Fogarty (Eds.), *If minds matter: A foreword to the future, Volume II* (pp. 275–280). Palatine, IL: IRI/Skylight Publishing, Inc.

de Bono, E. (1992). *Serious creativity.* New York: HarperCollins.

DeMott, B. (1990, March). Why we read and write. *Educational Leadership,* p. 6.

Dewey, J. (1938). *Experience and Education.* New York: Macmillan.

Diez, M. E., & Moon, C. J. (1992, May). What do we want students to know?...And other important questions. *Educational Leadership,* pp. 38–41.

Eisner, E. W. (1993, February). Why standards may not improve schools. *Educational Leadership,* pp. 22–23.

Ferrara, S., & McTighe, J. (1992). Assessment: A thoughtful process. In A. L. Costa, J. A. Bellanca, & R. Fogarty (Eds.), *If minds matter: A foreword to the future, Volume II* (pp. 337–348). Palatine, IL: IRI/Skylight Publishing, Inc.

Fitzpatrick, K. A. (1991, May). Restructuring to achieve outcomes of significance for all students. *Educational Leadership,* pp. 18–22.

Fogarty, R. (1992a). Teaching for transfer. In A. L. Costa, J. A. Bellanca, & R. Fogarty (Eds.), *If minds matter: A foreword to the future, Volume I* (pp. 211–223). Palatine, IL: IRI/Skylight Publishing, Inc.

Fogarty, R. (1992b). The most significant outcome. In A. L. Costa, J. A. Bellanca, & R. Fogarty (Eds.), *If minds matter: A foreword to the future, Volume II* (pp. 349–353). Palatine, IL: IRI/Skylight Publishing, Inc.

Fogarty, R., & Bellanca, J. A. (1987). *Patterns for thinking: Patterns for transfer.* Palatine, IL: IRI/Skylight Publishing, Inc.

Fogarty, R., Perkins, D., & Barell, J. (1992). *The mindful school: How to teach for transfer.* Palatine, IL: IRI/Skylight Publishing, Inc.

Frazier, D. M., & Paulson, F. L. (1992, May). How portfolios motivate reluctant writers. *Educational Leadership,* pp. 62-65.

Frender, G. (1990). *Learning to learn: Strengthening study skills and brain power.* Nashville, TN: Incentive Publications.

Fusco, E., & Fountain, G. (1992). Reflective teacher, Reflective learner. In A. L. Costa, J. A. Bellanca, & R. Fogarty (Eds.), *If minds matter: A foreword to the future, Volume I* (pp. 239–255). Palatine, IL: IRI/Skylight Publishing, Inc.

Gardner, H. (1991). *Intelligences in seven phases.* Paper presented at the 100th Anniversary of Education at Harvard, Cambridge, MA.

Glasser, W. (1990). *Quality school: Managing students without coercion.* New York: Harper Perennial.

Glasser, W. (1986). *Control theory in the classroom.* New York: Harper and Row.

Goodlad, J. I. (1984). *A place called school.* New York: McGraw-Hill.

Hamm, M., & Adams, D. (1991, May). Portfolio: It's not just for artists anymore. *The Science Teacher,* pp.18–21.

Hansen, J. (1992, May). Literacy portfolios: Helping students know themselves. *Educational Leadership,* pp. 66–68.

Hebert, E. (1992, May). Portfolios invite reflection—From students and staff. *Educational Leadership,* pp. 58–61.

Herman, J. L. (1992, May). What research tells us about good assessment. *Educational Leadership,* pp. 74–78.

Herman, J. L., Aschbacher, P. R., & Winters, L. (1992). *A practical guide to alternative assessment.* Alexandria, VA: Association for Supervision and Curriculum Development.

Hetterscheidt, J., Pott, L., Russell, K., & Tchang, J. (1992, May). Using the computer as a reading portfolio. *Educational Leadership,* p. 73.

Hills, J. R. (1991, March). Apathy concerning grading and testing. *Phi Delta Kappan,* pp. 540–545.

Hodgkinson, H. (1991, September). Reform versus reality. *Phi Delta Kappan,* pp. 9–16.

Jeroski, S. (1992). Finding out what we need to know. In A. L. Costa, J. A. Bellanca, & R. Fogarty (Eds.) *If minds matter: A foreword to the future, Volume II* (pp. 281–295). Palatine, IL: IRI/Skylight Publishing, Inc.

Jeroski, S., & Brownlie, F. (1992). How do we know we're getting better? In A. L. Costa, J. A. Bellanca, & R. Fogarty (Eds.), *If minds matter: A foreword to the future, Volume II* (pp. 321–336). Palatine, IL: IRI/Skylight Publishing, Inc.

Jeroski, S., Brownlie, F., & Kaser, L. (1990a). *Reading and responding: Evaluating resources for your classroom. 1–3, Grades 4–6.* Toronto, Ontario, Canada: Nelson Canada. (Available in the U.S. from Bothel, WA: The Wright Group.)

Jeroski, S., Brownlie, F., & Kaser, L. (1990b). *Reading and responding: Evaluation resources for your classroom.1–2, Late primary and primary.* Toronto, Ontario, Canada: Nelson Canada. (Available in the U.S. from Bothel, WA: The Wright Group.)

Jervis, K. (1989, April). Daryl takes a test. *Educational Leadership,* pp.93–98.

Johnson, B. (1992, Winter). Creating performance assessments. *Holistic Educational Review,* pp. 38–44.

Jones, B. F., Palincsar, A. S., Ogle, D. S., & Carr, E. G. (Eds.). (1987). *Strategic teaching and learning: Cognitive instruction in the content areas.* Alexandria, VA: Association for Supervision and Curriculum Development.

Kallick, B. (1992). Evaluation: A collaborative process. In A. L. Costa, J. A. Bellanca, & R. Fogarty (Eds.), *If minds matter: A foreword to the future, Volume II* (pp. 313–319). Palatine, IL: IRI/Skylight Publishing, Inc..

King, J. A., & Evans, K. M. (1991, October). Can we achieve outcome-based edcuation. *Educational Leadership,* pp. 73–75.

Knight, P. (1992, May). How I use portfolios in mathematics. *Educational Leadership,* pp. 71–72.

Kohn, A. (1992). *No contest: The case against competition* (rev. ed.). Boston: Houghton Mifflin Company.

Kohn, A. (1991, March) Caring kids: The role of the schools. *Phi Delta Kappan,* pp. 496–506.

Krogness, M. M. (1991). A question of values. *English Journal, 80*(6), 28–33.

Larter, S., & Donnelly, J. (1993, February). Toronto's benchmark programs. *Educational Leadership,* pp. 59–62.

Lazear, D. (1991). *Seven ways of knowing: Teaching for multiple intelligences.* Palatine, IL: IRI/Skylight Publishing, Inc.

Lazear, D. (1991). *Seven ways of teaching: The artistry of teaching with multiple intelligences.* Palatine, IL: IRI/Skylight Publishing, Inc.

Madaus, G. F., & Kellaghan, T. (1993, February). The British experience with 'authentic' testing. *Phi Delta Kappan,* pp. 458–469.

Majesky, D. (1993, April). Grading should go. *Educational Leadership,* pp. 88–90.

Malarz, L., D'Arcangelo, M., & Kiernan, L. J. (1991). *Redesigning assessment: Introduction. Facilitator's Guide.* Alexandria, VA: Association for Supervision and Curriculum Development.

Marzano, R. J., & Costa, A. L. (1988, May). Question: Do standardized tests measure general cognitive skills? Answer: No. *Educational Leadership,* pp. 66–71.

McTighe, J., & Lyman, F. T. (1992). Mind tools for matters of the mind. In A. L. Costa, J. A. Bellanca, & R. Fogarty (Eds.), *If minds matter: A foreword to the future, Volume II* (pp. 71–90). Palatine, IL: IRI/Skylight Publishing, Inc.

Ministry of Education, Province of British Columbia. (1991). *Enabling learners: Year 2000: A framework for learning.*

Ministry of Education, Province of British Columbia. (1991). *Supporting Learning: Understanding and assessing the progress of children in the primary program: A resource for parents and teachers.*

NASSP's Council on Middle Level Education. (1988). *Assessing excellence: A guide for studying the middle level school.* Reston, VA: National Association of Secondary School Principals.

North Central Regional Educational Laboratory (NCREL). (1991a). *Schools that work: The research advantage.* (Guidebook #4, Alternatives for Measuring Performance). Oak Brook, IL: Author.

North Central Regional Educational Laboratory (NCREL). (1991b). *Alternative assessment: Policy beliefs.* No. 15 & 16. Oak Brook, IL: Author.

O'Neil, J. (1992, May). Putting performance assessment to the test. *Educational Leadership,* pp. 14–19.

Paulson, F. L., Paulson, P. R., & Meyer, C. A. (1991, February). What makes a portfolio a portfolio? *Educational Leadership,* pp. 60–63.

Perkins, D., & Salomon, G. (1992). The science and art of transfer. In A. L. Costa, J. A. Bellanca, & R. Fogarty (Eds.), *If minds matter: A foreword to the future, Volume I* (pp. 201–209). Palatine, IL: IRI/Skylight Publishing, Inc.

Pipho, C. (1992, May). Outcomes or "Edubabble"? *Phi Delta Kappan,* pp. 662–663.

Pipho, C. (1990, October). Budgets, politics, and testing. *Phi Delta Kappan,* pp. 102–103.

Redding, N. (1992, May). Assessing the big outcomes. *Educational Leadership,* pp. 49–53.

Rhoades, J., & McCabe, M. (1992). Cognition and cooperation: Partners in excellence. In A. L. Costa, J. A. Bellanca, and R. Fogarty (Eds.), *If minds matter: A foreword to the future, Volume II* (pp. 43–51). Palatine, IL: IRI/Skylight Publishing, Inc.

Schudson, M. (1972). Organizing the 'meritocracy': A history of the College Entrance Examination Board. *Harvard Educational Review, 42*(1), pp. 40–69.

Semple, B. M. (1992). *Performance assessment: An international experiment.* Princeton, NJ: Educational Testing Service.

Shavelson, R. S., & Baxter, G. P. (1992, May). What we've learned about assessing hands-on science. *Educational Leadership,* pp. 20–25.

Shepard, L. (1989, April). Why we need better assessments. *Educational Leadership,* pp. 4–9.

Simmons, W., & Resnick, L. (1993, February). Assessment as the catalyst of school reform. *Educational Leadership,* pp. 11–15.

Simon, S. B., & Bellanca, J. A. (Eds.). (1976). *Degrading the grading myths: A primer of alternatives to grades and marks.* Washington, D.C.: Association for Supervision and Curriculum Development.

Sizer, T. R., & Rogers, B. (1993, February). Designing standards: Achieving the delicate balance. *Educational Leadership,* pp. 24–26.

Spady, W. G., & Marshall, K. J. (1991, October). Beyond traditional outcome-based education. *Educational Leadership,* pp. 67–72.

Stefonek, T. (1991). *Alternative assessment: A national perspective: Policy Briefs.* No. 15 & 16. Oak Brook, IL: North Central Regional Educational Laboratory.

Stiggins, R. J. (1991, March). Assessment literacy. *Phi Delta Kappan,* pp. 534–539.

Stiggins, R. J. (1985, October). Improving assessment where it means the most: In the classroom. *Educational Leadership,* pp. 69–74.

Szetela, W., & Nicol, C. (1992, May). Evaluating problem solving in mathematics. *Educational Leadership,* pp. 42–45.

Tyler, R. W. (1949). *Basic principles of curriculum and instruction.* Chicago: University of Chicago Press.

U.S. Department of Labor. (1992, April). *Learning a living: A blueprint for high performance.* (A SCANS report for America 2000). Washington, D.C.: The Secretary's Commission on Achieving Necessary Skills.

Vavrus, L. (1990, August). Put portfolios to the test. *Instructor,* pp. 48–53.

Vickery, T. R. (1988, February). Learning from an outcomes-driven school district. *Educational Leadership,* pp. 52–56.

Wandt, E., & Brown, G. (1957). *Essentials of educational evaluation.* New York: Holt, Rinehart, and Winston.

White, N., Blythe, T., & Gardner, H. (1992). Multiple intelligences theory: Creating the thoughtful classroom. In A. L. Costa, J. A. Bellanca, & R. Fogarty (Eds.), *If minds matter: A foreword to the future, Volume II* (pp. 127–134). Palatine, IL: IRI/Skylight Publishing, Inc.

Wiggins, G. (1992, May). Creating tests worth taking. *Educational Leadership,* pp. 26–33.

Wiggins, G. (1989, April). Teaching to the (authentic) test. *Educational Leadership,* pp. 121–127.

Williams, R.B. (1993). *More than 50 ways to build team consensus.* Palatine, IL: IRI/Skylight Publishing, Inc.

Winograd, P., & Gaskins, R. W. (1992). Metacognition: Matters of the mind, matters of the heart. In A. L. Costa, J. A. Bellanca, & R. Fogarty (Eds.), *If minds matter: A foreword to the future, Volume I* (pp. 225–238). Palatine, IL: IRI/Skylight Publishing, Inc.

Wolf, D. P. (1989, April). Portfolio assessment: Sampling student work. *Educational Leadership,* pp. 35–39.

Wolf, D. P., LeMahieu, P. G., & Eresh, J. (1992, May). Good measure: Assessment as a tool for educational reform. *Educational Leadership,* pp. 8–13.

World-Class Standards...For World-Class Kids. (1991). Kentucky Department of Education. Information on 1991–1992 Assessments.

Worthen, B. R. (1993, February). Critical issues that will determine the future of alternative assessment. *Phi Delta Kappan,* pp. 444–456.

INDEX

There are

one-story intellects,

two-story intellects, and three-story

intellects with skylights. All fact collectors, who have

no aim beyond their facts, are one-story men. Two-story men

compare, reason, generalize, using the labors of the fact collectors as

well as their own. Three-story men idealize, imagine,

predict—their best illumination comes from

above, through the skylight.

—*Oliver Wendell*

Holmes